THE DREAM N

By the same author:
VISIONS OF THE FUTURE

THE DREAM MACHINE

Lucid Dreams and How to Control
Them

DR KEITH HEARNE

THE AQUARIAN PRESS

First published 1990

British Library Cataloguing in Publication Data

Hearne, Keith
The dream machine: lucid dreams and how to control them.
1. Dreaming. Parapsychological aspects
I. Title
135'.3

ISBN 0-85030-906-9

Cover illustration
Traces showing eye-movement signals made by the sleeping subject
as a response to electrical stimuli.

The Aquarian Press is part of the Thorsons Publishing Group, Wellingborough, Northamptonshire, NN8 2RQ, England.

Typeset by Burns & Smith Ltd., Derby

Printed in Great Britain by Woolnough Bookbinding Limited, Irthlingborough, Northamptonshire

1   3   5   7   9   10   8   6   4   2

This book is dedicated to Celia Green, whose timely scholarship prepared the way for the scientific exploration of lucid dreaming and the important discoveries about the general dream state that inevitably resulted.

Contents

Preface

Technology has greatly facilitated the scientific study of dreams. The basic physiological monitoring apparatus of a few decades ago, which so advanced our knowledge of dreaming sleep, has now progressed to the portable bedside dream machine that anyone may use at home. This unit can detect dreaming sleep when it occurs, and then waken the dreamer after a set period so as to increase dream recall. One version permits the user to attempt the experimental induction of 'lucid' dreams—in which the dreamer becomes fully aware of dreaming and can then control events in the dream.

As a result of the technological investigation of dreaming, we have at last begun to comprehend the true nature of dreams. In the past, dream theories tended to be established on some conjecture, which was neither provable nor disprovable. Now, though, we have discovered consistencies and facts, which theories have to encompass satisfactorily in order to survive.

Alarmingly, or excitingly (depending on one's viewpoint), the highly anomalous condition of lucid dreaming has thrown into question our current ideas of consciousness and reality. The possibility exists that even waking life is, in actuality, just a well-structured dream-type experience!

Keith Hearne B.Sc., M.Sc., Ph.D.
Hearne Research Organization
PO Box 180
Hull
North Humberside
HU1 2EW

1

Signals from another world

Breakthrough

I was in the Psychology Department's sleep-laboratory at Hull University; the time was seven minutes past eight on the morning of Saturday, 12 April 1975. After an all-night vigil by the recording apparatus, my eyes were half closed as I sat alone sleepily watching the ink traces on chart paper being churned out at 1.5 cm per second. The male subject had been in a dreaming period for nearly half an hour. Before going to sleep, the subject had been instructed to make a series of eye movements to left and right should he realize at any point that he was actually dreaming. That type of dream is termed a 'lucid' dream, and the subject had reported experiencing them quite often.

Suddenly, out of the jumbled senseless tos and fros of the two eye-movement recording channels, a regular set of large zig-zags appeared on the chart.

Instantly, I was alert and felt the greatest exhilaration on realizing that I was observing the first ever deliberate signals sent from within a dream to the outside. The signals were coming from another world—the world of dreams—and they were as exciting as if they were emanating from some other solar system in space. A channel of communication had been established from the inner universe of the mind in dreaming sleep.

From within indubitable dreaming sleep, with its well-defined characteristics of low-voltage brain waves, rapid bursts of patternless eye movements, and profound muscular paralysis, an intelligent message was being writ large via these ocular excursions. They were proclaiming: 'I have become aware that I am asleep and dreaming. I am in a dream environment, but I know that my body is wired up in the sleep-lab and that you are in the control room waiting for these signals.'

It may be difficult for some people who have never experienced dream lucidity to believe in the phenomenon. It is more than just a vivid dream—it is like being awake but knowing full well that you are in a dream-scape. Normally in dreams comprehension is limited; we accept nonsensical situations without question, and the dream is considered retrospectively on waking. In lucid dreams, however, full critical awareness can arise. At the moment that the period of dream lucidity (which can last several minutes) starts, a transformation takes place; it is as if consciousness has been suddenly switched on. You are aware of who you are, your personal history, and that your body is really home in bed. You can pick up objects and inspect them minutely, and even question persons around you. Rather than being swept along by the dream, you observe what is happening with cool insight and intelligence. The artificiality of the dream surroundings is realized, but the 'realness' is so striking that the whole experience can be one of sheer wonderment!

Backgrounds

Ever since reading Freud's *The Interpretation of Dreams*,[1] as a teenager, I have been hugely interested in dreams. The first experimental work that I performed in the area was to investigate 'hypnotic' dreams, when an undergraduate at Reading University in 1973. I discovered a way of externalizing the imagery of these dreams[2] (Chapter 4).

On obtaining my degree in psychology from Reading, I was keen to pursue those experiments for a Ph.D., and was offered a place at several universities; I chose Hull. It soon became apparent, however, that 'hypnosis' was not necessary in the procedure I had used. The subjects all had exceptional abilities in visualization. We all differ in this ability. Some people on hearing a high-imagery noun such as 'aeroplane' instantly 'see' a vivid, coloured, detailed picture of an aircraft, whereas others (I am one) cannot visualize anything at all. Most people's experience is somewhat between those two extremes.

The results of the original study are quite valid, however, since they provide data about the imagery process—which is likely to be the same for nocturnal dreams.

At that time, some new computer equipment was installed at the Psychology Department in Hull, and I thought of a novel way of investigating visual imagery—the basis of dreams—using a technique measuring 'visually-evoked responses' (VER).[3, 4] Essentially, if a light is flashed into your eyes, an electrode placed over the visual cortex of the brain (at the back of the head) will respond with a characteristic complex wave-shape. The size and position of the different peaks vary according to certain conditions, such as the surrounding brightness.

The idea came to me that if two groups of subjects (poor and good visualizers) were used and they attempted to image a bright scene, the VER in the good imagers should have a lower measure than in poor imagers, because of the background 'brightness'. There were several other variations on that theme in the study.

It was the sort of research that results in more questions than answers. The findings were uncertain because so many variables were involved. For instance, the two groups were probably not equally motivated. The poor imagers were probably very bored (since they could not visualize scenes), and this may have affected the VER in any case. Experimental psychology can be very complicated!

While this work was continuing, I was also busying myself with several parapsychological experiments using the sensitive new equipment.[5] Additionally, I was becoming proficient at the physiological techniques in sleep research and becoming engrossed in computer programming. It was a marvellous period of having full and free access to the new research facilities. My wife, Patty, and I were happy, and there were many pleasant dinner parties, visits to places, and the occasional wild party. Life was lived to the full!

Many students would drop in at our flat in central Hull, and there were hours of discussion on every conceivable topic. Dreams were frequently raised, including the 'lucid' sort.

It struck me one day that lucid dreams really were of immense importance. Because of the unique feature of consciousness accompanying dreaming, it might be possible to use these dreams to study the dreaming process itself *from within*.

REM and SWS

Dreams are particularly associated with REM (rapid eye

movement) sleep, which emerges about every 90 minutes. REM sleep alternates with slow-wave sleep (SWS). The first nightly REM period lasts only a few minutes, but at each appearance the duration increases so that, by morning, a REM period may be over half an hour long. REM sleep has certain identifying features. The brain waves show 'low-voltage', mixed frequency activity: there are occasional sequences of random REMs; breathing becomes shallow, quiet, generally faster than in SWS, and a little irregular; the body's musculature is paralysed, except for breathing (otherwise we would act out our dreams!); erections are present in males and there is evidence of clitoral enlargement in females.

REM is embedded within a matrix of SWS, which is arbitrarily divided into four stages. On going to sleep, Stage 1 is first encountered. The polygraphic chart shows slow rolling eye movements in many subjects, a loss of any waking 'alpha' brain waves (about 10 cycles per second activity), and a lessening muscle tonus. Stage 2 is noticeable by its 'K-complexes', which

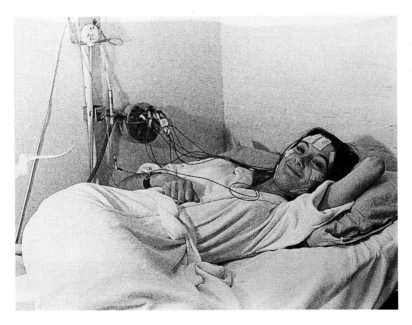

Fig. 1.
A subject wired up for sleep-monitoring in the sleep-laboratory

happen in the brain waves (EEG) in response to any sudden external or internal stimulus—such as a noise. Brain waves become more synchronized and of higher voltage in Stages 3 and 4. Stage 3 is defined as having 20 to 50 per cent slow waves of a certain amplitude, and Stage 4 has over 50 per cent.

In order to remember a dream, it is necessary to awaken—even briefly. It is interesting to consider that we dream for a total of perhaps two hours each night, but only a small fragment is recalled in the morning. In the course of a lifetime we spend several years in that inner world!

Fig. 2.
The author at the polygraph recorder

The experiment

One of the people I knew was a man of 37, A.W., who years previously had acquired a degree in psychology but who now co-ran a second-hand shop in Hull. He also did removals, and that is how Patty and I met him, when we moved house. A.W. said that he had lucid dreams.

I determined to conduct some experiments with lucid-dream subjects in the sleep-laboratory, and A.W. volunteered. The main thought in my mind was whether it would be possible to signal somehow from inside the dream, on becoming lucid.

Charles Tart, the well-known American psychologist and parapsychologist, had wondered whether a two-way communication system between subject and experimenter could be developed so that instructions and reports could be signalled.[6] He pointed out that such a step would change the status of the dream from a subjective event, reported retrospectively, to a more immediate form of behaviour. He asked whether subjects could incorporate certain stimuli so that these could act as signals to direct the subject to perform specific activities in dreams. He believed that simple motor acts, such as raising a finger, could be performed, and he also considered the possibility of subjects using 'automatic writing' or 'sleep talking'. Celia Green, in her excellent book *Lucid Dreams*, had also suggested training subjects to make movements in sleep.[7]

A major difficulty, however, with such notions is that there is massive muscular inhibition during REM sleep, as those who have ever experienced 'sleep paralysis' on waking from dreams will appreciate. It was anticipated that lucidity would emerge from that type of sleep, so I doubted that the subject could signal reliably—if at all—say, by pressing a micro-switch taped to the hand. The subject did say that he woke spontaneously, or could rouse himself with effort, from a lucid dream, but scientifically a subjective report of having 'just had a lucid dream' would not be acceptable. It might have been that memory was distorted during sleep.

Micro-switches had been used in a few previous experiments concerning ordinary non-lucid dreaming. In one study,[8] subjects were told to press the switch whenever they thought they were in dreaming or non-dreaming sleep. However, the authors admitted that the signals obtained were usually associated with signs of waking. In another experiment,[9] it was stated that a simple 'jerk' response could be elicited to a tone stimulus in REM sleep, apparently with no signs of waking, particularly if punishment for failure to respond was introduced. However, such unconscious actions are hardly comparable to deliberate, thought out movements. I decided to try using the micro-switch method with my lucid-dream subject, but a new technique was really required.

It flashed upon me one day that since the eye musculature is obviously exempt from the general atonia of REM sleep (by definition), it might be possible for the subject to make volitional ocular movements as a method of signalling. A few days later, the subject was 'wired up' in the usual manner for monitoring brain waves, eye movements and muscle activity. Both methods of signalling would be used, so a small micro-switch was taped to the subject's hand. The instructions were simple. On becoming aware of being in a dream, the subject was to make a sequence of about eight eye movements to left and right, as smoothly as possible, and also press the micro-switch several times. Both actions would show clearly on the chart record.

The first night of this test was an anticlimax. The recording apparatus was switched off for the night at 8 a.m. after continuous all-night monitoring. Unfortunately, it seems that the subject had a lucid dream shortly afterwards while I was folding up some chart paper and generally clearing up. He reported on waking that he had attempted to signal by both techniques.

A week later, the first signals from 'inner space' were received. By coincidence, it was the anniversary of man's first orbit in 'outer space' by Yuri Gagarin on 12 April 1961. In the dream, just before lucidity, the subject was walking around the university wearing electrodes. The novelty of the situation suddenly made him think, 'I'm dreaming,' and he immediately signalled. Several other sets of eye signals were communicated and the dream scenery itself was largely ignored on this first occasion.

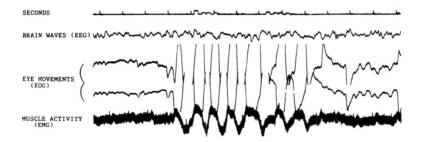

Fig. 3.
First ever ocular signals from a lucid dream

Thus, a scientific tool became available, for the first time, for studying dreams from the inside. The seemingly insuperable problem of bodily paralysis had been circumvented and a new field of research was ready for exploration.

Interestingly, a few months later, on sending details of my technique to Dr Allan Rechtschaffen, the eminent researcher into sleep and dreams at Chicago University, he replied most encouragingly and also mentioned that he had obtained some eye signals from a patient having an attack of sleep paralysis. He'd

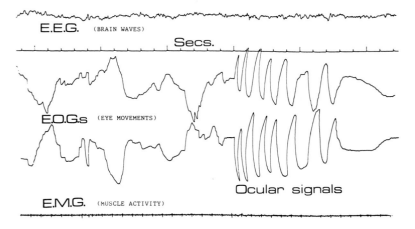

Fig. 4.
Signals recorded at Liverpool University, 1976

come up with a similar answer to essentially the same problem (that of muscular atonia).

Aware of the very great possibilities for making discoveries that could shed considerable light on the dreaming process, I decided to abbreviate my work on VERs and imagery, submit it for an M.Sc. degree, and start anew on a Ph.D. project concerning lucid dreaming. A change of city was considered and an application made to the Psychology Department of Liverpool University; it was accepted.

Discoveries

The new signalling technique was ideal for establishing some basic criteria about lucid dreaming (and dreaming generally).

The signals were, in effect, 'event markers' that could identify specific episodes in the dream and be registered on the chart record. Nothing comparable had ever been possible before. In addition, certain consistencies became apparent on comparing the lucid-dream chart records, and these provided a basis for theorizing about how lucidity is caused.

In the first lucid-dream study, using A.W. as the subject, eight complete lucid dreams were recorded polygraphically.[10]

A mass of data was collected. All the lucid dreams were in indisputable Stage REM sleep, demonstrating that they were definite dreams rather than a version of waking imagery. The duration of this subject's lucid dreams (measured from the onset signals to spontaneous waking) varied from 1 to 6 minutes, with an average length of 2½ minutes. They usually happened between 6.30 and 8 a.m., when REM sleep was plentiful, and appeared, on average, 24 minutes after the start of an REM period.

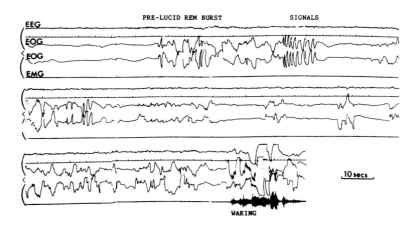

Fig. 5.
Polygraphic record of a lucid dream

A major discovery was the consistent observation that lucidity was invariably preceded by a burst of REM activity lasting an average of 22 seconds. A reasonable explanation perhaps is that the burst of activity from the base of the brain that causes REMs also 'prods' the cortex to a level where parts of one's long-term memory are 'switched on' again (having been disconnected at sleep onset), so giving access to adequate information about oneself.

One simple yet important thing that the research showed was that the dream is not 'over in a flash'—probably the most popular misconception about dreams. The lucid dream was operating in 'real' time. Apart from the initial lucidity onset signals, other events (e.g. a period of flying) were marked—before and after—by similar coded eye movements. These events were evidently taking up dream time, and the estimates of dream duration were in close agreement with actual time.

Also, it was confirmed that the dream report is an accurate statement of what was experienced, within the ordinary limits of short-term memory. Dream reports accorded with the evidence on the chart record. The sequence of events described later correspond with those signalled. There was no distortion or 'secondary revision' in the recollection process.

The lucid dreamer can certainly think coherently and has access to recent memories. The subject could carry out instructions stated to him before he went to sleep.

There was a strong indication that the emotional level in the lucid dream was 'pre-set' by that brain stimulation that causes REMs. Heart rate in the lucid period was highly correlated (0.87) with duration of the pre-lucid REM burst (where a correlation of 1 represents perfect correlation and 0 means no correlation). This is potentially a highly relevant factor in trying to reach an understanding of dreams.

In one lucid dream, the subject was giving a running commentary but, of course, the muscular atonia of REM sleep prevented any sound actually being produced. He could 'hear' his own voice clearly but nothing came over the intercom, and the EMG record, monitoring muscular activity, remained inactive.

There seemed to be symbolic material in some of the lucid dreams, referring to the experimental situation. In the early experiments at Liverpool, a noisy air-conditioning system could have influenced the subject's dream of a 'high wind'. In another lucid dream there was mention of a restraining 'wire grille' above the subject's head, which may have represented the mass of electrode wires. In another lucid dream, the subject thought he was being observed by someone behind a window. There was a window between the sleep-lab control room and the bedroom.

Here, then, was an almost embarrassing abundance of completely original information that fully revealed the basic parameters of lucid dreaming, and also provided some interesting ideas about dreaming generally. Obviously, the door to a fascinating new field of science had been unlocked.

Just testing

One of the sobering lessons that I learnt from my previous work on 'hypnosis' was that subjects will go to great lengths to comply with the experimenter's stated or implied wishes. It was with that in mind that I decided to run a 'stimulating control' experiment, just to see whether subjects could produce signals like the ones I had observed, by deliberate deception. Perhaps a subject who woke in the night could produce an REM-like polygraphic record and make eye signals in a way that was indistinguishable from the real state. I needed to know for my own satisfaction.

Nine subjects were employed in the study. They were told: 'Some people claim to have dreams in which they realize they are dreaming. At those times they also claim that they can signal to the experimenter by moving their eyes from left to right eight times, simultaneously pressing a button eight times. However, it could be that they are really awake then. Your task is to produce the same behaviour by pretending or faking it in any way you like, whenever you wake in the night. Sometimes you will be woken from dreaming by me saying 'signal' quietly. On hearing this, remain quite still for a few seconds, then signal.' These instructions, purposely devaluing the original work, gave free reign to subjects to produce the same results, then, by cheating.

An independent judge selected the most REM-like records from each subject, and these were then given to four further judges, with a randomly selected sample of the lucid-dream subject's signal record (a different one for each judge). These judges were provided with the standard scoring criteria for Stage REM sleep and asked to pick out any showing those features.

Reassuringly, each judge deemed that only the actual lucid-dream record met the scoring criteria, thus supporting the genuineness of the original results. In addition, all the simulating subjects pressed the micro-switch, which the real subject could not manage to do because of sleep paralysis in REM.

Personal confirmation

I began researching lucid dreams without ever having experiencing one. However, on 28 July 1976 the first one came. It was absolutely incredible, and made me realize, very strongly, the tremendous potential of the dream state.

In the dream, I was wandering along on some rocks by the seaside, which seemed to be the Mediterranean. People were laughing and playing in the sunshine. I looked into the shallow water and thought I could make out some old pieces of metal in the water. Next, the sea was gone and I was digging out some coins.

Suddenly, I realized that this was a wish-fulfilment situation that I had experienced before in dreams. I said 'aloud' to myself, 'This is a lucid dream!,' and stood up and looked around. It was a wonderful dawning of consciousness. I was now observing everything with full awareness. I observed that the colours were much deeper than normal and that perspective was not that of wakening life.

I noticed a tightness around my eyes and even considered making the eight eye-movement signals as practice, but did not do so as there would be no evidence.

Remembering the controllability aspect of lucid dreams, I decided to make a girl appear and that she should resemble someone I once knew. There was a stack of deck-chairs about 20 feet away. I walked up to them, all the while thinking 'this is taking up a lot of dream time', and expected to see the girl behind the chairs, but no one was present. I was disappointed at this inability to control the dream, but suddenly I noticed a girl walking towards me. She was short and dark-haired, which fitted the required description.

I was wondering whether to introduce myself, when she smiled at me and said, 'Hello.' I took her hand and we walked off happily together. I asked her name. She replied, 'Jane.' She had green eyes and a perfectly symmetrical face. We suddenly found ourselves in Birkenhead and we were looking for the home where she was born. Explosions were heard nearby—perhaps it was war-time bombing. I sensed that the dream was ending. Jane was sitting on a flight of stairs at a factory. In a poignant scene, I held both her hands and promised I would return to see her. She smiled beautifully. I then awoke. Initially, the dream was perfectly lucid but as it developed into a fantasy situation the sharpness of that lucidity declined somewhat.

Strangely, I met a girl, about three weeks after the dream, who was short and dark-haired, with green eyes and a very pretty, symmetrical face. Her name was Jane and she was identical to the girl in the dream!

A second study

A further set of experiments were undertaken with the subject, to extend the findings. Various manipulations, such as using external stimulations, were included in the sleep-lab work, and relevant data from other sources were collected for analysis (lucid-dream frequency, diary information and questionnaire data).

One significant physiological discovery made in the sleep-lab in this study was that the subject could voluntarily alter his breathing rate. Clearly, the respiratory musculature was not affected by inhibition in REM sleep. Another mode of communication from within the lucid dream was thereby established.

On one occasion three separate sets of eye signals were obtained from the subject in slow-wave sleep, as distinct from REM, showing that signalling can occur in that state too, but imagery was probably lacking.[11]

The subject made a careful record of his lucid dreams over a 170-day period from 1 August 1976. For part of that time a questionnaire was filled in after each lucid dream, and a diary was kept of each day's events. There were 36 lucid dreams in that period. They cropped up on any night of the week with roughly equal frequency, but there seemed to be a periodicity effect with this subject in that a quarter of the lucid dreams happened four days after a previous one. The maximum duration between lucid dreams was 12 days.

The diary data was entered hourly, when possible. Three independent judges rated how active those days had been before a lucid dream, as compared to control days. However, no statistically significant effects were noted.

Data from 29 of this subject's lucid dreams were combined in a questionnaire. Bearing in mind that the information is subjective and possibly unique to the subject, it was found that the brightness and clarity of images did not alter after the onset of lucidity, and that clarity of thought, emotionality, and bizarreness did increase from that moment. This last point was unexpected, but it could be that on attaining lucidity bizarre features may be thrown into higher relief with the input of consciousness to the dream.

These, then, were the major findings with the first lucid-dream subject. A host of ideas for other experiments bombarded me, but it was time for reporting some results.

Publication

An invitation was extended to me to read a paper on the research at the 11th Post-graduate – Post-doctoral Conference in the Behavioural Sciences in mid-April 1977, at Hull University. It was most gratifying to return to Hull, where the signalling technique was discovered, and present full details of my findings to an interested audience of academics, including Dr Donald Broadbent, F.R.S., of Oxford University.

The scientific establishment took some convincing about the research results. It seems that the 'experts' were rather caught out—a not surprising fact to me at the time since, in my own experience, most sleep and dream researchers were completely ignorant of lucid dreaming, and there was hardly any literature on this topic. A paper based on the one given at Hull University was sent to *Nature*. A reply received on 9 June 1977 stated that 'in the Editor's opinion the paper would not command wide enough an audience in the scientific community'(!). The editor of *Psychophysiology*, Harold Williams, Ph.D., rejected a paper. It was very obvious that some referees 'did not comprehend the research. Eventually, though, at other journals, scientists who knew about lucid dreaming insisted on publication: 'This is an important and timely paper, and should definitely be published.'

There was more interest from the media. Newspapers and local radio stations had been interested in the work since 1976 when the signalling technique was publicly described. A broadcast on the BBC's World Service, in April 1977, brought in a large quantity of post from several countries. A technical article on the findings appeared in the *Nursing Mirror*[12] and a scientific paper was published in the *Journal of the Society for Psychical Research*.[13] Subsequently, many other papers and articles were published. The research was particularly well received at the Annual Conference of the Society for Psychical Research at Brighton in 1980. The notion of lucid dreaming had arrived![14]

Invention

Necessity is the mother of invention. A trite phrase, but it was quite true in the case of the motivation behind my inventing the 'dream machine'. The notion arose originally in my mind because of the inefficiency of the method I was employing in obtaining data on lucid dreams. The subject I was using had a lucid dream on a minority of nights spent in the sleep-laboratory, so there was much wasted time.

While still at Hull University, I'd had the idea that it might be feasible to construct some kind of 'dream machine' that would induce lucidity artificially. The more the notion was cogitated upon, the more possibilities I saw for such a device. It could also increase ordinary dream recall, alleviate nightmares, and would have other potential functions too.

So far as lucidity induction was concerned, such a device would consist of some form of dream detector, various timers, and some method of applying to the dreamer an external stimulus that would be perceived within the dream without causing waking. Since lucidity is usually initiated as a consequence of noticing some flagrant inconsistency in the dream scenery, a standard 'external cue' might be very effective.

Incorporation

Sometimes we weave into our dreams stimuli that are emanating from the world of wakefulness. The noise from an alarm clock may be converted to some other sound, perhaps as someone shouting. Sleep-laboratory studies have looked at this phenomenon of incorporation.

Berger (1963)[15] found that spoken names could be incorporated into the dream, often in a distorted fashion. Thus, Naomi became 'an aim to ski' in the dream report, and Jenny was transformed to 'jemmy'. Dement and Wolpert (1958)[16] tried stimulating subjects with a tone, light, and water-spray. Incorporation amounted to 9, 23 and 42 per cent respectively. Clearly, there were ways of penetrating into the dream state.

Experimentation was called for in the quest for a lucidity-generating stimulus.

The search

A method that I tried at Hull involved speaking, or playing, the sentence 'This is a dream' to the subject when the polygraphic record was tracing out the physiological evidence of REM sleep. It was not found to be successful.

At Liverpool, the pressures to invent a 'dream machine' became stronger, because I was spending so much time wastefully in the sleep-laboratory. I developed a virtually permanent reversed sleep pattern—sleeping in the day. This was fine for the research, but it put a limit on my social life and my marriage was being very adversely affected.

One sleep-lab study that was undertaken tried to initiate lucidity in subjects by means of a water-spray. Subjects were asked to produce a pattern of eye signals, which would be monitored in the chart record if such realization was present. A 'control' condition was included in the experiment, using a 'catch' trial (when no stimulus was applied) in order to ascertain whether subjects were merely trying to please the experimenter. In many psychological experiments, subjects often feel obliged to behave so as to comply with the experimenter's desires. 'Hypnosis' is the most notorious area for this effect.[17]

Ten subjects, mostly females, were used in the study. They spent two nights in the lab, the first being an 'adaptation' night to get used to the situation. The instructions to subjects were these: 'On two separate occasions tonight, when you are dreaming, some water will be sprinkled lightly on your face. As a result, you may dream, say, that it is raining, or that a pipe has burst and has sprinkled you. What you have to remember is that if you dream of being sprayed in any way, it is a signal to you. You should then realize that you are dreaming. You must then immediately signal back by making six eye movements to left and right, while simultaneously pressing the micro-switch six times.'

I entered the subject's bedroom and used a syringe to spray the water during the actual trials. During the control trials, I entered the bedroom with a syringe but applied no spray. In either condition, the subject was then woken and asked for a dream report.

In 6 out of 10 subjects, a clear link with water was present in the dream report for the experimental trials. There were no such mentions in the control trials.

Trial summaries of dream reports:

1   Dream of washing a baby and getting splashed.
2   Dream of speaking to a friend who was inadvertently spitting.
3   Dream of being on a yacht, with spray on face.
4   Dream of 'thinking what to say'.
5   Dream of taking an exam.
6   Dream of watering plants in the sleep-lab, and water dripping from washing hanging above the bed.
7   Dream of standing on pavement, wiping wet shoes on dry grass.
8   Dream of a black cat which I had let into the sleep-lab. It urinated on the subject.

The results demonstrated a high incorporation of the water-spray stimulus, but the expected lucidity was not forthcoming.

I even constructed an apparatus, which I used at home, consisting of a timer linked to a motor with a fast-rotating paddle that was placed in a bowl of water. It sprinkled water over my face after a pre-set time. This Heath Robinson arrangement was not successful.

Another study used olfactory (smell) stimuli. Perfumes, cloves and other pungent stimuli were administered to subjects, but here incorporation was low. Yet another experiment used a simple tone signal sounded in REM, but this was not found to be effective in eliciting lucidity.

Koulack's study

My perseverence in seeking a workable lucidity-generating technique was rewarded when I came across a paper by David Koulack,[18] who was describing work performed at the Department of Psychiatry in the State University of New York. Dr Koulack was not investigating lucidity induction at all, but he found that electrical pulses given to the wrist, above the median nerve, were incorporated into dreams more frequently than any other type of excitation.

He used 10 subjects, who were woken up three times from a control condition (where no stimulation was administered) and three times from each of four experimental conditions when stimulation was given. The four experimental conditions varied the time into the REM period when the pulses were sent, and the length of time the subject was permitted to dream after stimulation.

The study was, essentially, psychiatric and designed to test some hypotheses derived from Freudian theory. These expectations were not confirmed in the work, but the main significance to me was the effectiveness of stimulus incorporation. Sometimes the pulses were perceived directly in the dream:

> The thought was I felt a pinch in my hand. Electrical impulse. With this electrical impulse I was awake and I got up out of bed and I sat near a desk. I looked at the time and it was five o'clock and I went back to bed again. And the phone rang and I realized it was just a dream.

This subject had, in fact, a 'false awakening' (dreaming of being awake).

Sometimes the pulses entered the dreams indirectly:

> I dreamt ... that I had a snake on my bed in the lab, and uh ... it was a long black snake, and uh, I had to call you up because I didn't know what to do.

In the condition where stimulation happened three minutes after detection of the first REM, and the subject was roused three minutes later, there was 24 per cent indirect incorporation and 40 per cent direct—making a satisfactory total of 64 per cent inclusion of the electrical pulses.

Here, then, was a simple, electronically easy way to administer stimulation to the subject that would present itself to the mind during dreaming.

The technique, meant now for lucidity induction, was first tested in the sleep-laboratory at Liverpool University. It produced only false awakenings in the first subject, but research a little later showed that lucidity could indeed be initiated by the method. Eventually, a study using 12 subjects found that half of them became dream-lucid (Chapter 6).

Dream detection

All this time, I had in my mind the concept of a small, portable, bedside 'dream machine', capable of several functions including experimental dream-lucidity induction, and which could be used by anyone at home. Such a unit would, naturally, require some kind of dream detector to determine when the electrical pulses should be administered. The search for that element of the overall invention went alongside that for a suitable stimulus but proved to be more difficult to attain than was at first imagined.

There are several bodily phenomena associated with REM sleep, and perhaps the most obvious one is the presence of REMs. The first automatic dream detector that I designed was intended to identify REM sleep by monitoring ocular movements. The device was termed 'CEMOS'—an acronym for 'coded eye-movement operated switch'—and was constructed by the workshop at Liverpool University according to my specifications.

It worked after a fashion sometimes but on the whole was not at all satisfactory. Movements caused false signals and subjects were not too happy about applying electrodes to their face. In fact, two American researchers[19] also worked on such a device, but it too had problems.[20]

After experiments with several methods (some highly eccentric!) that attempted to monitor physical or physiological correlates of REM sleep, a very sensitive and reliable way was chosen. It is that of detecting respiratory rate by means of a nasal thermistor (heat detector). The respiratory rate in REM is elevated compared to that of SWS. A small bead-thermistor is simply taped to the side of the nose so that the bead is positioned in the air flow. A fine, flexible wire goes to the top of the bed so that it does not impede the subject's movement. The temperature of exhaled air is warmer than inhaled air, and this difference is easily measured even if mouth breathing is occurring.

The marriage of that technique, which has an automatic method of electrical stimulation, with the addition of electronic timers, gave birth to the world's first 'dream machine'. Patents were applied for and granted.

Publicity

There is something about the concept of a 'dream machine' that strikes a universal chord. Most people know what fantastic experiences can occasionally occur in dreams, and to realize that more such episodes can be recalled, and that dream consciousness and controllability are also possibilities for them, rouses a natural curiosity about the topic. There is a potential in the dream state that most of us instinctively know can be tapped, and here was a way of assisting in attaining that goal.

Nevertheless, I was fairly surprised by the immense media focus on the device. As soon as news of the invention reached the news agencies, there was immediate and widespread interest. I was besieged with callers. On one day, hardly anyone could get through to the University of Hull (where I had returned as a Post-doctoral Research Fellow) because so many reporters were trying to reach me. Countless radio and TV items appeared, along with newspaper and magazine articles all over the world.

Bandwagon

In retrospect, I suppose it was inevitable that the dream machine would attract con-men, hangers-on and various other unscrupulous characters. Various superficially plausible and not so plausible persons approached with all kinds of appealing propositions which, on inspection, were not to my advantage. One man turned up with a hand-written legal document and wanted me to sign over the rights to the invention for £1, so that he could become my 'agent'! Several very nasty people crawled out of the woodwork, all attracted by the perceived financial potential of the device. I was more interested simply in helping people to learn how to dream.

Perspective

There is something deeply pleasing about having conducted original research, and especially in producing an invention that has a great potential for mankind. Certainly, the dream machine will evolve with technical advances, but its basic principle will be the same as that of today's device. Everyone dreams, and that state can be detected and interrupted. In addition, external stimuli can enter dreams and, in some people, be recognized as cues that one is dreaming. These are universal facts.

One very clear observation from this perspective of time is that the inventive idea was only a small part of the very long and arduous process of developing and testing a new device, and getting it manufactured and launched. Motivation is perhaps even more important than creativity in successful invention. Looking back, that original research was remarkably productive—but then, it was a completely virgin field. The basic electrophysiological and psychological characteristics of lucid dreams were established. Later excellent work by La Berge, Gackenbach and others in the USA fully confirmed those discoveries.

References

1. Freud, S. (1955, orig. 1900) *The Interpretation of Dreams*. Basic Books, New York.
2. Hearne, K.M.T. (1973) Some investigations into hypnotic dreams using a new technique. B.Sc. thesis, University of Reading.
3. Hearne, K.M.T. (1975) M.Sc. thesis, University of Hull.
4. Hearne, K.M.T. (1975) Visual imagery and evoked responses. *Psychological Research*, **40**, 89–92.
5. See *Journal of the Society for Psychical Research* (1977–81).
6. Tart, C. (1965) Toward the experimental control of dreaming: a review of the literature. *Psychological Bulletin*, **63**, 87–99.
7. Green, C. (1968) *Lucid Dreams*. Institute of Psychophysical Research, Oxford.
8. Antrobus, J.S., Antrobus, J.S. & Fisher, C. (1965) Discrimination of dreaming and non-dreaming sleep. *Archives of General Psychiatry*, **12**, 395–401.
9. Williams, H.L., Morlock, H.C. & Morlock, J.V. (1966) Instrumental behavior during sleep. *Psychophysiology*, **2** (3), 208–16.
10. Hearne, K.M.T. (May, 1978) *Lucid dreams: an electrophysiological and psychological study*. Published Ph.D. thesis, University of Liverpool.
11. Hearne, K.M.T. *ibid*, 241–2; 405 (record).
12. Hearne, K.M.T. (1980) Insight into lucid dreams. *Nursing Mirror*, **150** (1), 20–22.
13. Hearne, K.M.T. (1981) 'Lucid' dreams and ESP. *Journal of the Society for Psychical Research*, **51** (787), 7–11.
14. Hearne, K.M.T. 'Lucid dreams: a new area for psi investigation'. Annual Conference of the SPR (1980).
15. Berger, R.J. (1963) Experimental modification of dream content by meaningful verbal stimuli. *British Journal of Psychiatry*, **109**, 722–40.
16. Dement, W.C. & Wolpert, E. (1958) The relation of eye movement, body motility, and external stimuli to dream content. *Journal of Experimental Psychology*, **55**, 543–55.
17. Orne, M.T. (1962) On the social psychology of the psychological experiment: with particular reference to demand characteristics

and their implications. *American Psychologist*, **17**, 776–83.

18. Koulack, D. (1969) Effects of somatosensory stimulation on dream content. *Archives of General Psychiatry*, **20**, 718–25.
19. Goldberg, R.M. & Beiber, I. (1979) A portable REM-detecting machine. *IEEE Transactions on Biomedical Engineering*, **BME-26** (9), 513–16.
20. Beiber, I. (1981) Personal communication.

2

Wakenings

Dream recall can be increased very substantially by the expedient of waking the subject from successive REM periods. People using a bedside dream machine at home are woken automatically when the device electronically responds to the respiratory features characteristic of REM sleep. Waking is achieved by means of a not unpleasant audible alarm which begins softly and gradually increases in volume, so gently rousing the dreamer. A short-timer, which in one version can be set by the user, starts counting when dreaming is detected. On its completion, the waking alarm is activated. This feature of the device enables a reasonable length of dreaming to have been experienced before interruption. In some cases, the user may wish to be woken immediately at emotional peaks in dreams. For such experiments, the short-timer is set to zero.

A separate long-timer may be set, which determines when the device becomes operational. In the first half of the night there is little REM sleep. Slow-wave sleep predominates in the sleep cycle. Therefore, the user may set the device so as to have several hours of uninterrupted sleep before the unit starts to function. On the other hand, some users are interested in noting differences and similarities between dreams from different REM periods, and so set the long-timer to a low value or to zero.

Overriding all these features, and constantly monitoring throughout use, is a nightmare-detector function—designed to protect the user. It detects the higher respiratory rate associated with nightmares and would cut in immediately to sound the waking alarm should a pre-set value be exceeded.

So as not to disrupt the user's sleep pattern too much, it is generally recommended that the device should not be used every night. Some 'dream freaks' are tempted to do this. Individuals should find out by trial and error the amount of usage best suited to themselves.

Triggering

With one version of the device, subjects were asked to conduct an experiment to find out the optimum respiratory-rate setting for themselves. They were instructed to set the device's respiratory-rate control to a different randomly selected figure, between a wide range, each night. Details were noted in a log about whether a dream was in progress each time the subject was woken. By this method, the best 'triggering' rate for that individual could be ascertained. The following is a typical log report:

RECORD OF 8 OCCASIONS OF USING DREAM MACHINE IN 'NIGHTMARE' MODE
(DREAM MACHINE EXPERIMENT 2)
The fixed breathing rate setting you must use for each night is given in column C. If the figure is too low, and continual waking occurs, select a value of your own choosing instead. Note down the new figure in column C.

A Date	B a. BED TIME b. GET UP TIME	C BREATHING RATE SETTING	D RECORD OF EVENTS CONCERNING DREAM MACHINE
20/7/87	a. 11 pm. b. 7.00 am.	24	1. 3.40 woken by device was dreaming. 2. 4.30 Woken by device. Dreaming.
22/7/87	a. 11.30 pm b. 7.30 am.	30	1. } No awakenings. 2. }
23/7/87	a. 11.00 pm b. 7.00 am	26	1. 3.50 am Woken by device. Dreaming. 2. 4.30 am Woken by device. Was dreaming.
25/7/87	a. 10.45 pm b. 7.00 am	18	1. 2.50 am Woken by device. NOT dreaming. 2. 3.00 am Woke by device. Not dreaming.
28/7/87	a. 11.40 pm b. 7.00 am	28	4.10 am Woken by device. Dreaming. No further awakenings.
30/7/87	a. 10.30 pm b. 7.00 am.	22	1. 2.05 am Woken by device, dreaming. 2. 2.50 am Woke by device. Not dreaming.
2/8/87	a. 10.30 pm b. 7.00 am	32	} No awakenings
5/8/87	a. 10.45 pm b. 7.00 am.	20	1. 2.25 am Woken by device. Not dreaming. 2. 2.45 am Woke by device. Not dreaming.

Fig. 6.
Subject's log

Clearly, with this subject, settings of 28 and over were too high. No triggering occurred with those values, so no awakenings happened. Settings of 18 to 22 were too low, resulting in false triggering from non-REM sleep. Values of 24 to 26 were suitable for this person.

Immediate waking

One study of dream machine users collected examples of dreams where the waking alarm sounded immediately the optimum triggering breathing rate was attained. These wakings, at slight emotional peaks, were quite interesting. These are cases from different subjects.

Time: 3.45 a.m. Setting: 30

It is the end of the working day. It is night-time. I am waiting, with my fellow workers, to clock off, but outside at the top of the factory I see an open window. I am slightly annoyed that I may have to go back and close it when I want to get away. Seconds later it is shut from the inside. That is good.

'Ready for the off,' I say. 'Time to go. They're off and running.'

I run to the car feeling slow and stiff. I think how fit and healthy trainers must make a horse for a race. In the car I have a little trouble finding reverse gear. I drive to the road, turn left and just miss a managing director's car. He is with his family and is parking on my left. I just manage to flash my acknowledgement. Up the road I bear to the right on my way home. I feel I am just a little too fast, but in control. At this point the alarm wakes me.

The setting of 30 was high, and it is not surprising that some fairly active behaviour was going on in the dream for the device to trigger at that value. The level probably built up over a few minutes. Running to the car was almost certainly associated with an elevated breathing rate, and the near-accident would have upped the rate even further. The sensation of being in a car going too fast produced the rate necessary to trigger the machine.

Speculatively, one might see signs of symbolic verbal associations guiding the dream. From nearly hitting the managing director's car, the dreamer, on waking, is only just managing to direct the car.

Time: 6.50 a.m. Setting: 22

I was walking into a house. Music was coming from a chest of drawers. I 'knew' that each compartment or drawer can be changed to another section so causing the sound to change. I am trying to decide how to change the volume, when I am woken.

This is a more usual respiratory rate setting for subjects. There seems to have been some excitement about the novel piece of furniture, and this was linked to an increasing breathing rate. Symbolically, the object might represent the dream machine. It too has several functions or compartments and produces sound (the audible alarm).

Time: 5.18 a.m. Setting: 22

I, as a little boy of about 12, was talking to my folks in a one-room cabin in the woods in one of the western states of the United States, and I got into an argument with my dad. He said that something wasn't true and I said it was. After what seemed like a few minutes, I jumped out of an open window and dropped a few feet to the grass below. I ran into the moonlit night toward the mountains. I soon came upon a black horse in a clearing in the woods and started talking to it—I don't know what I said—while brushing the horse with a hand-held brush. There seemed to be sawdust scattered over the front of the horse and I brushed it off from the top of his face, which had a white marking, to his back and his legs. Then I woke.

This subject's breathing rate increased only slowly despite quite an amount of emotional and physical happenings in the dream. The final scene with the horse, though, caused the device to sound the waking alarm—for unfathomable reasons.

Time: 5.20 a.m. Setting: 22

I was in the lounge with two friends. Without knowing why, I was shaking a bottle of whisky. As I shook it, it began to froth, and when I put it down, it continued to do so. I felt the frothing and foaming looked like a storm in miniature, and I knew the bottle was going to explode. I got down on the floor and hid behind something, and worried about my friends. They too were on the floor. The bottle exploded, covering us in whisky, and one of my friends said, 'The place smells like a brewery.' The bottle exploded a second time and damaged a wall and the room was flooded with water. I began to worry about drying the walls and imagined doing it with an electric fire—at the same time wondering if I'd have to strip off the wallpaper I had only just decorated the walls with.

A Freudian analysist would doubless pontificate much about such a dream, but there are so many unknown factors here that no definitive explanation is possible.

Time: 7.38 a.m. Setting: 20

I was driving east around behind a racquetball club and noticed that the road was very bumpy in places, but that parts had been repaired by being asphalted. I noticed a friend's car parked there, and then I curved around the road and headed back west. I wondered what my friend was doing at the club, as it was early morning. I then saw my friend walking along the sidewalk. I stopped my car and rolled down the window. I then asked him how he was doing. He replied, 'Not so good, I've been sick.' I said, 'I'm sorry to hear that.' I was just getting ready to ask him if it would be all right for me to bring another friend along with me to the Friday afternoon work-out when I heard the beeping of the machine. I thought of the machine for a split second while I was in the dream and then awoke.

This was a type of wish-fulfilment dream, because in waking life the dreamer was wanting to meet a friend to ask him if it would be all right to bring someone new to the work-out. Possibly the alteration in respiratory rate, linked to 'speaking' in the dream, triggered the unit.

Time: 9.20 a.m. Setting: 20

I am walking along the streets of a city at night with two friends—a man and a woman. I know the woman in real life, but the man I do not know. The night-life is quite active. The man and I leave the woman on a street corner and walk on until we find ourselves in front of a shop which specializes in electronic games. We become fascinated by one, which resembles football in that a ball is thrown across an enclosed area. When the ball rolls near our end of the table, we can work a lever which bats it across the table again. After a while, we realize we have forgotten all about the woman. We walk back to find her, but cannot see her. A group of skaters come by; they're all adults. A voice somewhere tells us that a new breed of human being is being created. This is where I woke up.

This is a low breathing-rate setting and the device is activated by what would seem to be fairly mild anxiety.

As always with observations of human behaviour, there are vast individual differences in responses to certain conditions. Some people seem to have extremely unemotional dreams, whereas others are vividly engrossed in James Bond type escapades each night!

Validation

In the sleep-laboratory, electrophysiological recording of subjects has demonstrated what happens to cause the home dream machine to 'trigger'. In addition to being wired up to the portable bedside dream machine, the subject is also attached via many electrodes to a multi-channel chart recorder. The change in respiratory pattern from SWS to REM is noticeable in the chart record, and the moment at which the device is activated can be clearly identified. Essentially, it provides evidence that the unit is actually triggering in REM sleep.

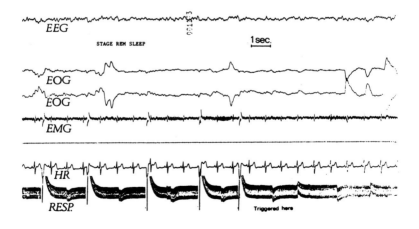

Fig. 7.
Polygraphic record of a subject attached to the dream machine. An increase in respiratory rate in Stage REM (dreaming) sleep has caused the device to trigger. Waking, by an incrementing audible alarm, occurred after a set delay of several minutes

The following are typical examples (shortened) from subjects brought into the sleep-lab for one night, not having used a dream machine before. The long-timer was set at 4 hours, so that no awakening occurred before that period had elapsed.

Subject: C.R. (male)   Setting: 28

4.20 a.m. 'Quite a clear dream. I actually dreamed I was awake and couldn't sleep! I wanted to move to another bed in the sleep-lab and was about to call you.'

5.20 a.m. 'A vivid, but very confused dream.'

6.50 a.m. 'A very vivid dream. There were lots of people. I was in a bank and people were being searched. One suspect was being searched. They couldn't find the loot. He had stuck it up his arse!'

Subject: P.G. (female)   Setting: 25

4.35 a.m. 'I dreamed I was getting angry with someone. I was saying, "Keep your hands off." '

5.55 a.m. 'A clear dream in which I was standing in the street waiting for someone on a bicycle.'

7.15 a.m. 'A fairly vivid and coloured dream. I was standing in a bus queue with some old ladies. One wore a blue and white dress. I commented on her outfit.'

8.05 a.m. 'A vivid dream. I was in my house. It had a spare room. There was a fire in a factory at the back of the house. My son Paul aimed a hose at things in a garden to sweep them away and protect them from the fire.'

Subject: A.K. (female)   Setting: 25

4.12 a.m. 'A vivid dream of being in prehistoric times.'

5.38 a.m. 'A vivid dream about my family. We were having fun and playing around.'

7.03 a.m. 'I was dreaming vividly about telling a group of people at the college where I am a student about this experiment. The director was there. People were interested and amused.'

Studies like this have confirmed that the device's respiratory monitoring system is without doubt effective and reliable at identifying REM periods during sleep. They validate the basic operation of the dream machine.

The American researchers Aserinsky and Kleitman[1] noticed in 1953 that the respiratory rate was generally higher in REM than in SWS sleep. Variability in breathing was reported by Snyder et al. in 1964.[2] Following my own research, Peter Paepe of Belgium tells me that he became interested in the topic and conducted research into respiratory changes during sleep. The very title of his doctoral thesis is a confirmation of the dream machine's basic operation: 'Validation of an REM sleep detector based only on respiration rate'.

Using a computer system linked to a polygraph, Paepe measured 'inter-breathing intervals'. A special computer program searched the continuous flow of data for any set of parameters that he specified. He found that there were individual differences between subjects, as I had in my research. REM sleep could be detected with 100 per cent reliability in one subject with just two inter-breath intervals of under 3 seconds, whereas another might take five successive measures to attain 100 per cent reliability.

Basically, Paepe managed to get total reliability at REM detection simply by monitoring multiples of the 3-second or less inter-breath period. The dream machine operates on a similar principle. This independent academic support for the device's operation helped its credibility in scientific circles.

These results demonstrate that my method of automatically detecting dreaming sleep by its characteristic breathing changes and then, after a variable period, of waking the dreamer or administering some kind external stimulus is now scientifically verified and established.

Dream interpretation and analysis

Several analysts have realized that the dream machine is a tremendously valuable tool for furthering research into dream interpretation. The device, being capable of extracting data from different REM periods in the night, and of differing emotional quality, provides an immense opportunity for theorists to test old ideas or come up with new ones.

For instance, it is often found that the dreams of one night all centre on a common theme (e.g. water). The significance of that theme can only be discovered by inspecting a sequence of dream reports from that night. It is anticipated that considerable work will be undertaken in the future concerning dream analysis using the device as a data-gathering aid.

For the impartial researcher too, not subscribing to any one belief system about dreams, the area is full of potential.

The means is now at hand to advance our knowledge of dreaming more than ever before. Vast strides will be made.

Nightmares

One of the most useful functions of the dream machine is to alleviate the problem of nightmares. Surveys indicate that nightmares, operationally defined as frightening dreams that awaken the dreamer, may be present on a once-a-week frequency in about one in 20 of the population.[3] That means that there are very many millions of people in the world who suffer from this unpleasant sleep disorder. Some people experience them more often, sometimes every single night. It is then that sleep becomes terribly aversive. I have been contacted by some individuals so frightened to go to sleep that they had become literally suicidal. For some sufferers that problem is overwhelming; for others it is a nuisance that is upsetting and adversely affects one's mood during the next day.

It is surely the case that nightmares are responsible for some fatalities in sleep. The massive physiological strain accompanying a nightmare has undoubtedly resulted in cardiac arrest in some sufferers. Anyone who has woken from a severe nightmare, with racing heart, panting, and copious sweating, will understand the medical dangers of the phenomenon.

There are two types of nightmare, each linked with the two distinct sleep states: SWS and REM. Slow-wave sleep nightmares are rare. Fisher et al.[4] found that they constituted only about 4 per cent of the total. They mostly occur within the first hour and a half of sleep, when SWS is most abundant. This type is not preceded by any physiological signs. The person wakes suddenly, absolutely panic stricken, often screaming or calling for help. Breathing then becomes rapid and there is a fast heart rate. I recall monitoring one case in the sleep-lab. The female subject, a student, was sleeping soundly in Stage 4 sleep. Suddenly a frightened, and frightening, scream came from the bedroom, I dashed in, to find the girl sitting upright in bed in great distress. After several minutes she settled down again and went back to sleep. In the morning she had no recall at all of the incident.

Gastaut and Broughton[5] suggested that SWS nightmares result from a disturbance in the arousal system. It has been observed that a sudden noise can precipitate the phenomenon. I have proposed[6] that in situations where sudden noises could exacerbate the problem the sufferer should adopt the simple expedient of using ear-plugs. Fisher et al. stated that the SWS nightmare sufferers they investigated had been 'traumatized', say by witnessing violence in their homes during childhood.

The great majority of nightmares are anxiety dreams which happen in REM sleep. These are nearly always preceded, for several minutes, by increases in physiological measures, e.g. respiratory rate, heart rate and eye movements. The normal muscular paralysis of REM sleep may be reflected in some nightmares where the dreamer is unable to move.

What is it like to have a nightmare? The following accounts from my files should illustrate the unpleasantness of these nocturnal episodes:

Female: Frequency: variable—sometimes several per night

> I always wake up screaming, petrified and very often crying. My husband can usually hear me 'building up to a scream' and tries to gently wake me before I reach screaming point. I think I am usually running away from someone or something, or trying to catch someone or something. I sometimes call for my mother or husband, but usually let out blood curdling screams. I remember recently dreaming that my husband and I were about to be stabbed. In my most recent nightmare I woke up screaming when a large stone fountain was spraying liquid chocolate at me!

It should be noted that the woman's husband, in waking her gently before the dream's climax performs the function of the nightmare-interruptor feature of the dream machine, although the device could almost certainly detect signs of distress at an earlier stage.

The same nightmare theme keeps recurring in some sufferers:

Female   **Frequency: 4 per week on average: 95% recurring theme**

My boy-friend (Roy) is coming home from work down the lanes on a tractor, very late at night. My ex-boyfriend (Paul) is driving behind him in a Lancia—overtaking and obstructing the tractor so that Roy has to stop. Roy then gets out of the tractor and politely asks Paul to move. He gets out of his car, and stabs and shoots Roy. I find his mutilated body on the doorstep in the morning. I scream and wake up crying.

Encountering the same nightmare repeatedly often leads to recognition of the situation and realization of dreaming. This insight could be utilized to alter the dream in anyone who knew about techniques of dream control. The sufferer linked to a dream machine need only make a few rapid breaths to trigger the nightmare-interruptor alarm—resulting in being 'beamed up' to the waking world. The following account is from someone who would benefit from having a dream machine.

Female   **Frequency: 1 per 3 weeks on average; 75% recurring theme**

I am in a house. There is a room that I know contains something terrible. The room is always at the top of a flight of stairs, on the right. The stairs are narrow, steep, dark and musty. I have to go past this room, and always find myself having to go in. On one occasion the room tricked me into thinking it was another room and when I went in it changed into the room I fear. The atmosphere in the room is always intense and frightening, and sometimes stays with me all day after waking. I always know that I'm dreaming, but I can't wake myself up. The dream is very vivid and I can remember the details and colours easily. I have had the dream since I was about 4 years old.

The medical danger associated with some nightmares is highlighted in the next report:

Male   **Frequency: 1 per week on average**

My nightmares are mostly about someone I knew several years ago. During the nightmare I have severe differences of opinion with him which develop into violent quarrels to such an extent that I awake with severe chest pains reminiscent of my first heart attack. I am completely exhausted and find this very frightening in the middle of the night.

Survey

I conducted a survey and personality study of 39 frequent-nightmare sufferers who responded to an appeal. They were nearly all females, having an average age of 35 years. This female preponderance could be because of a 'response bias' in that males may be more reluctant to report having nightmares, and/or it may be the case that females are more susceptible to the problem. The age of onset was most frequently reported to be in the first 10 years of life. Six out of 10 subjects thought that a trauma had preceded onset. In this particular group, the peak frequency for nightmares was about three per week. Nine out of 10 subjects had nightmares that recurred some or all of the time, and nearly half said they were scared of going to sleep.

The most striking finding—one that had been overlooked or ignored in other studies—was that REM nightmares emerge, mostly, in the first half of the night's sleep. It is surprising, because most REM sleep happens in the second half. This strongly indicates that it is unlikely that purely psychological factors cause nightmares. The great variety of dream images in the second half of the night should surely touch upon sensitive themes by chance and set off nightmares if they were just psychologically-based. That is unless a psychological 'pressure' builds up and causes early nightmares and the resulting 'tension reduction' ensures that the energy is usually insufficient to reactivate another episode later that night. However, if night-mares were merely the venting of accumulated emotion, they would release most energy first, on being triggered, and then decline in intensity. That is the opposite to what is reported by sufferers and what is demonstrated by polygraphic studies.

It seems more reasonable to hypothesize that at sleep onset the anxiety-sensitivity threshold becomes steadily lowered, and this state persists for a while into the following REM period. The sufferer becomes more 'jumpy' as it were. Possibly, as the amount of SWS declines in each 90-minute cycle, the susceptibility to nightmares becomes reduced.

It is possible to envisage that with the lowered anxiety-sensitivity threshold a slightly scary dream image or thought could evoke an inordinate response, increasing in intensity as associations with previous nightmare situations are added and so leading to a full-blown nightmare. The idea agrees in many ways with the arousal-disorder theory of Gastaut and Broughton. The evidence is that nightmares are physiologically based, occurring in anxious people. This view is backed up by the observation that nightmares may suddenly appear in cases of drug-related 'REM rebound'. (Many drugs abolish REM sleep, but the body develops 'tolerance' and REM is restored gradually. However, when the drug is discontinued 'REM rebound' results, with a disproportionate amount present in sleep.) It is not reasonable to suppose that persons who stop taking drugs simultaneously become psychologically unstable and prone to 'meaningful' nightmares.

The pre-sleep level of anxiety is likely to be an important baseline. The very anticipation of having a nightmare, in frequent sufferers, must be sensitizing—as might be a preceding trauma. Anything that reduces the level of anxiety before sleep is likely to be therapeutic. The real effect of behaviour-modification treatments for nightmares may be more to do with the reduction of the overall level of anxiety about sleep than the desensitizing of specific nightmare situations.

The nightmare themes in 38 samples from sufferers could be classified thus:

A   Witnessing horror (10) and violence (2)
B   Experiencing attack (8) or danger (3)
C   Flight from someone or something (5)
D   Sinister presence (5)
E   Being late and frustrated in travel (2)
F   Suffocation (1)
G   Hallucinating creatures (1)
H   Paralysis (1)

The thematic analysis of nightmares revealed the main categories to be either where the sufferer was on the receiving end of violence or was shocked by witnessing violence. However, the psychological content may not be so important if physiological factors are mainly responsible for 'driving' the nightmare. The assumption that, because a nightmare is accompanied by great emotion, the psychological events experienced must therefore have been causative and 'meaningful' is not sound.

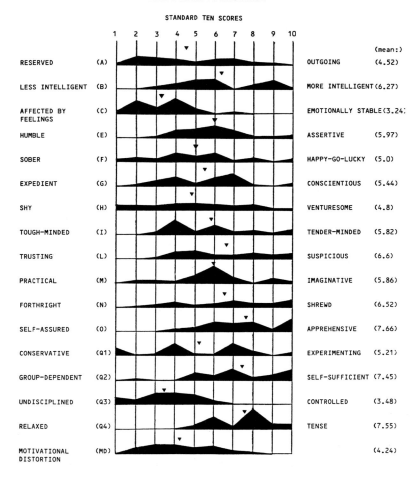

Fig. 8.
Frequencies of 16PF scores and mean test scores of nightmare sufferers

Fig. 8 shows the 'mean personality profile'[7] of 29 of the subjects in the study. The most outstanding features were, in descending order:

Factor C: affected by feelings
Factor O: apprehensive
Factor Q4: tense

Factor Q3: undisciplined
Factor Q2: self-sufficient

There may well have been a response bias here, but it superficially supports the idea that anxious people have nightmares.

The medical model

When looking at 'causes' of psychological problems, it has often been assumed that the 'medical model' should be applied. Thus, a phobia, say, or a nightmare, might be regarded as a 'symptom' resulting from some psychological 'disease'. In medicine, successful treatment of the disease relieves the symptoms. The psychoanalytic approach to treating a phobia might be to seek out some basic, hidden 'disease'. However, it is possible to eliminate phobias using behaviour-modification techniques. For example, a spider phobia can be overcome by the psychologist presenting a spider closer and closer each visit to the client, and linking the creature with a reward. It is tantamount to treating successfully a medical illness by just dealing with the symptoms! Clearly, the medical model is not appropriate for such areas. The modern psychological approach is to view phobic behaviour as a maladapted habit, which can be 'unlearnt'.

Similarly, with nightmares, the problem can be eliminated without searching for any 'cause'. Nightmares are not some kind of safety valve. They do not have to 'run their course'. Behaviour modification works with nightmares. For example, Geer and Silverman[8] treated a 22-year-old man who had experienced a recurring nightmare for 15 years. The client imagined the fearful events while simultaneously relaxing and thinking 'it's only a dream'. The therapy lasted 13 sessions, after which the nightmare was completely extinguished. There was no evidence of 'recidivism' or 'symptom substitution' after six months. Several other successful cases have been reported by various workers.

The dream machine and nightmares

The poet Coleridge, who was badly afflicted by nightmares (no doubt largely due to his predilection for opium), stated that the only respite he ever had from them was when he stayed with the Wordsworths at Dove Cottage. There, someone would sit up all night watching him* for signs of distress and then gently wake him. That, essentially, is what the dream machine (in the 'nightmare-interrupter mode') is intended to do, automatically and probably more sensitively. Once the respiratory rate equals a pre-set figure, the device activates the waking alarm instantly. The reassurance the unit provides to sufferers is immense. If the user knows that any nightmare will be 'nipped in the bud', then sleep is no longer aversive. The whole attitude of the sufferer can change dramatically. 'It is like having a guardian angel by the bed,' said one user.

Medically, there is not much that can be done about night-mares. In the survey data, most subjects stated that their prescribed medications were useless. Physicians can, however, now suggest the dream machine as a means of control. This aspect of the dream machine, which can bring about the relief of so much human suffering, and even save lives, is a great source of satisfaction to me as the inventor.

Asthma

Another condition which might conceivably be helped by the device, is asthma. In Britain, some 2000 people die each year of asthma attacks. These are often at night. The sufferer wakes up, after a period of increasingly difficult breathing, unable to breathe and panic stricken. A cardiac arrest may ensue.

It was accidentally discovered that asthmatics using the dream machine were pleased with the device because it woke them before a full attack was upon them. The users could then self-administer their bronchodilatory inhalers and the consequences of a full episode were averted. One well-known person who is also an asthmatic, who reported the asthma-alleviating effect, is the British entertainer and writer Michael Bentine. If the effect of the device is merely psychological, in giving reassurance and comfort to users of being 'watched over in sleep', it is still beneficial and therapeutic.

References

1. Aserinsky, E. & Kleitman, N. (1953) Regular periods of eye motility and concomitant phenomena during sleep. *Science*, **118**, 273-4.
2. Snyder, F., Hobson, J.A., Morrison, D.F., & Goldfrank, F. (1964) Changes in respiration, heart-rate and systolic pressure in human sleep. *Journal of Applied Physiology*, **19**, 417-22.

3. Feldman, M.J. & Hersen, M. (1967) Attitudes toward death in nightmare subjects. *Journal of Abnormal Psychology*, **72**, 421–5.
4. Fisher, C., Byrne, J.V., & Edwards, A. (1968) NREM and REM nightmares. *Psychophysiology*, **5**, 221–2.
5. Gastaut, H. & Broughton, R. (1965) A clinical and polygraphical study of episodic phenomena during sleep. In *Recent Advances in Biological Psychiatry*, ed. J. Vostis, Vol. 8, Plenum Press, New York.
6. Hearne, K.M.T. (1980) Terror lurking in the dark. *Nursing Mirror*, **151** (7), 18–20.
7. Cattell, R.B. & Eber, H.W. (1967) Sixteen personality factor questionnaire. *Institute for Personality and Ability Testing*, Illinois.
8. Geer, J.H. & Silverman, I. (1967) Treatment of a recurrent nightmare by behaviour modification procedures. *Journal of Abnormal Psychology*, **72**, 188.

3

Behold! It is a dream!

The notion of conscious, controllable, or 'lucid' dreaming has only become established as a widespread concept in the public domain in recent years. Before that, even many sleep and dream researchers were ignorant of the phenomenon! The literature on the topic consisted mainly of a few anecdotal accounts from individual writers who had personal experience of that type of dream. The area has been remarkably and surprisingly neglected, presumably because most of the theorists on dreaming were not aware of them. The story might well have been very different had Freud, say, been a frequent lucid dreamer.

The Marquis Hervey de Saint-Denys

The Marquis Hervey de Saint-Denys wrote a book,[1] *Les Rêves et les moyens de les diriger*, published in 1867, in which he related his experiences and observations about his own conscious, controllable dreams. An oriental scholar, he made meticulous notes on his dreams and discussed them with intelligent insight.

At the age of 13, Saint-Denys began to have dreams in which 'I was conscious of my true situation'. Fascinated by this paradoxical phenomenon, he would wrench himself from sleep after a dream and record details of what happened. It became his desire to produce a complete theory to describe the dreaming process. His collection of dream notebooks covered a period of 1946 nights, and he made numerous coloured illustrations in them of dream images. After six months of regular dream-book exercise, Saint-Denys was recalling dreams every night. On the 207th night, Saint-Denys had a 'lucid' dream—and again a week later. After six months, these arose about two nights out of five, and after 15 months he was dreaming lucidly each night. Saint-Denys was now in an excellent position to comment on dreams as a skilled introspectionist.

Saint-Denys believed that dreams essentially represent underlying thoughts. If you think of something in a dream, it will appear in the dream scenery. The basis of the images is previous perceptions, so that nothing is seen in the dream which has not actually impinged on the retina, even though it may have been forgotten. A dream may have precise images, but any vague elements are so because the original image was unclear.

Saint-Denys provided the interesting example of a dream in which he visited Brussels, a city he had never been to in waking life. Everything was clear, and he saw the well-known church of Saint-Gudule in the distance. He made a particular point of inspecting a shop in a street, and woke himself to write down all the observed details. Months later he visited Brussels but found no sign of the shop. However, several years later, Saint-Denys was in Frankfurt and found that same shop. He had been there previously, when a teenager. The dream had combined familiar pictures of the church with memories of a street in a different city, from years ago. Probably, there was some association of ideas between the two sources.

As an illustration of the flow of ideas in dreams, Saint-Denys cited a dream in which he was watching a bull-fight where a fighter was mortally wounded. He next found himself in Normandy, where he once saw an angry bull. Among the new peaceful country scenery, though, lay the body of the toreador. Saint-Denys thought this combination of images was presented because the powerful image of the dying toreador took longer to fade from his mind.

Sometimes two ideas can appear simultaneously and constitute one cause of bizarreness in dreams. A process may transfer some feature from one pictorial element to another. Saint-Denys gave as an example a dream of an emaciated horse drawing a cart, with the idea apparently being transferred to the farmer, who appeared thin and gaunt.

Another associative notion that he propounded was that of 'similarity of form', which, too, can result in bizarre images. Thus, an object can be transformed into something visually similar, such as a spinning dancer into a bobbin.

In addition to this natural flow of ideas in the dream, Saint-Denys pointed out that external and internal stimuli could affect

the dream and set off other avenues of association. In one chapter
of his book, Saint-Denys gives numerous examples of the incorporation of external stimuli into his dreams. He was insistent
that sensory thresholds were lower than during wakefulness,
although the cases cited are not terribly convincing.

He commented on the body's internal sensitivity during
dreaming, and mentioned that certain illnesses in him seemed to
be preceded by specific dreams. Headaches followed the dream
of climbing mountains with great facility. Saint-Denys noted that
some drugs, like morphine, produced stereotyped images. This
biochemical link is indeed fascinating and patently relevant to
any theory of dreams and to any school of dream interpretation.

Saint-Denys described one dream of his which appeared to
illustrate the effects of internal stimulation on content. In waking
life he had injured his shoulder. In the dream there were several
allusions to that shoulder. He took this repeated reference as
proof that painful stimulation continued in dreaming. It must be
stated, however, that the thought itself, prominent in his mind at
that time, might have caused the multiple references.

The various anomalies of memory in dreams intrigued Saint-
Denys, for instance, the phenomenon of dream events being
remembered better in subsequent dreams than in intervening
wakefulness. One night he dreamed of witnessing a quarrel
which resulted in a murder. He woke instantly, but the memory
drained rapidly. After some weeks, he had another dream in
which he had to give evidence about the murder and recalled the
events perfectly.

Can someone who is asleep and dreaming really reason
logically and exercise free will? Saint-Denys expressed positive
certainty on these matters.

To illustrate that intelligent, logical thought exists in the dream
state, he gave as an instance a dream where he was visited by a
relative whose wife was seriously ill. Saint-Denys was reluctant
to ask whether the caller's wife had died, so he started a
conversation and casually went over to where the caller's hat
had been placed, so that he could observe whether it had a
mourning-band.

In another dream, which happened at a time when Saint-Denys
was ill, he saw some medicine set out beside the bed. He
suddenly realized that the cup had, in fact, been broken the
previous day. The thought made him become aware of being in
a dream. He knew he would have to wake himself up to actually

take the medicine. However, he reflected that sleep was also important for him—so he decided to continue dreaming.

Of course, trying to determine whether reason and free will exist in dreams puts one in the same position as deciding whether similar qualities exist in waking life. One assumes affirmatively, but in both states there may be some degree of self-delusion. Rather than Saint-Denys's reason and judgement operating, was the dream process really urging him to stay asleep?

Saint-Denys discussed at length the effects of transformation and transition in dreams. Based on his observations, it seemed to Saint-Denys that natural associations in dreams were of two types: (a) from the chronological order in which memories are stored, and (b) abstractions.

Taking the first category, Saint-Denys gave the example of a dream where he was at a table with his family, with the diocesan bishop and two mythological divinities. Saint-Denys traced the associations back to a few days before the dream when he had been translating a piece from Ovid's *Metamorphoses* and was instructed to change his old jacket for a better one since the bishop had arrived and was to have lunch. The dream had been based on memories laid down at the same time.

Saint-Denys resorted to performing experiments in external stimulation to test his theories of association in dreams. In one enterprising experiment, for the whole duration of a two-week holiday in Vivarais, Saint-Denys constantly used a specific, novel scent and discontinued its use upon his return. Some months later, a servant who habitually entered Saint-Denys's bedroom at an early hour sprinkled some of the scent on the pillow. The morning had been randomly chosen by the servant. Saint-Denys had a vivid dream of being once again at Vivaris.

The success of this experiment motivated Saint-Denys to conduct others using several different scents, sometimes in combination. The experimental details are not really adequate to judge how scientifically sound these studies were. For instance, the close proximity of the servant might have been detected and itself have caused a dream on an expected subject. Nevertheless, to some extent, his examples indicate the operation of a dream process proceeding by associative pathways of various kinds.

In one 'combined-scents' experiment, Saint-Denys was caused to have a dream of Vivarais. He and his family were having dinner with his host and family when the door opened and his former art teacher entered with a naked model. The model's nakedness was not a matter of concern for anyone present and Saint-Denys noted sagely another associative effect—that dream images are produced from memory along with the feeling first registered in memory. Saint-Denys had seen this model before, in the matter-of-fact atmosphere of the artist's studio.

Saint-Denys went to more extreme lengths when he decided to experiment with auditory stimuli. He paid an orchestra leader to play one of two original waltzes each time he danced with one or other of two women. After this 'coincidence' happened many times, Saint-Denys had some musical-boxes made which played those tunes. The boxes could be linked to a silenced alarm clock, so that they could be played towards morning. He reported that the musical-boxes engendered dreams about the appropriate woman!

In a further experiment, on taste stimuli, Saint-Denys painted a canvas on the theme of Pygmalion. All the while he kept a piece of orris-root in his mouth. An assistant placed some of the substance between his lips while he was sleeping, at a later date, and a dream occurred which corresponded with the story.

Saint-Denys distinguished between primary and secondary ideas in dreams. Key thoughts or sensory stimuli were of the former type, and the mind's developments on those bases constituted the latter type.

'Transformation' occurs when a newly introduced primary idea suddenly enters the mind. The dream process tries to include it via associative links, but, if the idea is too strong, a sudden change of direction will be manifested in the dream.

Another effect is that of 'retrospective illusion' which happens when a new idea needs, for logic's sake, an introduction. Suppose you are stung, while dreaming, by a mosquito. The dream attempts to weave a dream, but does it backwards—starting from the bite. A quarrel might have been in progress...a duel challenged...leading to a sword injury. The order of events, however, is reversed on waking: 'Sometimes the thought precedes the sensation; sometimes it is the sensation that precedes the thought.'

The second type of associative process that Saint-Denys noticed in dreams was that of abstraction, where individual elements of a perception may be isolated and developed. Abstraction in wakefulness was different from that in sleep. When awake, the mind could pass from one subject to another without confusion. In dreams, the mind might be diverted by a particular element and this itself could generate the next scene, and so on. There could be sudden apparent changes in course, but based on associations using abstractions.

He listed two types of abstraction. The first was concerned with sensory effects. As an example, he saw in a dream an angry little dog which he saw 'rolled up'. He put his foot on it to 'roll' the creature. This action made him think of a 'roller' and he then found himself rolling a large flute. The dog's barking was replaced by music, which led him to a fête. Saint-Denys pointed out that this seemingly incoherent sequence of images had, in fact, a very logical basis of associations.

Verbal pathways were present in dreams. Saint-Denys met a girl in a dream. He asked her name and she replied, 'Sylvia.' Instantly, he found himself in a thick forest (Latin: *silva*) and the girl had become an attractive bird perched on his shoulder.

The second variety of abstraction consisted of those 'of a purely abstract order', that is, abstract ideas such as justice, generosity, pity, inequality, etc. Thus, a portrait of St Peter could give rise to the idea of religiosity, which might be transferred onto some pious person known to the dreamer. In this class, he also included the phenomenon where the dreamer can change from being a spectator to an actor, or vice versa.

To give an example, he dreamed that he witnessed a quarrel between two people. He sided with one of them and thought of what to say if he were in his place. Immediately, he became that other person in the dream.

Sometimes both types of abstraction may occur. Saint-Denys saw himself in the courtyard of an inn where thoroughbred and draught horses were drinking from a trough. The abstract idea of inequality came to his mind, and some lead pipes, which had previously been of the same proportions, now appeared to be of unequal lengths.

Saint-Denys further noted that although dreams relied on memory images for their building material, imagination could modify those images. This process could account, for example, for the metamorphosis of a bush into a walking stick. Images could be substituted by an approximation technique, initiated by a directing thought.

It was unfortunate that Saint-Denys's book on dreams was not better known to other writers and theorists on dreaming. Freud, for example, mentioned that he had been unable to obtain a copy of the book. Saint-Denys's superior knowledge of dream processes, from direct insightful observation within dreams, was an invaluable asset. Had Freud been fully aware of this type of conscious, controllable dream—and its revelations about what happens in dreams—he would surely have been diverted from the views he propounded. Unfortunately, Freud's ideas inordinately affected the thinking of people concerned with dreams for several decades.

Frederik van Eeden

It was Dr van Eeden who introduced the convenient term 'lucid' dreaming for when the individual becomes aware of dreaming and can control the activities. The occasion was a meeting of the Society for Psychical Research, in London, on 22 April 1913, when he presented a paper entitled 'A study of dreams'.[2] Van Eeden had studied his own dreams, and had kept a dream diary since 1896. Of 500 or so dreams recorded, 352 were of the 'lucid' variety, so he, like Saint-Denys, was an experienced introspectionist.

He first experienced lucidity in 1897:

> I dreamt that I was floating through a landscape with bare trees, knowing that it was April, and I remarked that the perspective of the branches and twigs changed quite naturally. Then I made the reflection during sleep, that my fancy would never be able to invent or to make an image as intricate as the perspective movement of the little twigs seen in floating by. [Page 446.]

Incidentally, the great physicist Professor Ernst Mach also realized he was dreaming once, because he found the movement of some twigs to be 'defective'.[3]

To illustrate the clarity of thought and exercise of free will in the dream state, van Eeden related the following case:

> On Sept. 9th 1904, I dreamt that I stood at a table before a window. On the table were different objects. I was perfectly well aware that I was dreaming and I considered what sorts of experiments I could make. I began by trying to break glass, by beating it with a stone. I put a small tablet of glass on two stones and struck it with another stone. Yet it would not break. Then I took a fine claret glass from the table and struck it with my fist, with all my might, at the same time

reflecting how dangerous it would be to do this in waking life; yet the glass remained whole. But lo! when I looked at it again after some time, it was broken. It broke all right, but a little too late, like an actor who misses his cue. This gave me a very curious impression of being in a *fake world*, cleverly imitated, but with small failures. I took broken glass and threw it out of the window, in order to observe whether I could hear the tinkling. I heard the noise all right and I even saw two dogs run away from it quite naturally. I thought what a good imitation this comedy world was. Then I saw a decanter with claret and tasted it, and noted with perfect clearness of mind: 'Well, we can also have voluntary impressions of taste in this dream world; this has quite the taste of wine.' [Page 448.]

Unlike Saint-Denys, who thought that the senses were enhanced in sleep, van Eeden was convinced that external or bodily stimuli penetrated the dream only exceptionally. In fact, van Eeden defined the 'true dream' as 'that state wherein bodily sensations, be they visceral, internal or peripheral, cannot penetrate to the mind directly, but only in the psychical, non-spatial form of a symbol or an image'. He avoided using the term 'unconscious' in his writings because he didn't accept the concept.

He illustrated the lack of bodily sensation in dreams by referring to a lucid dream that he experienced whilst suffering pain:

In April 1906 I was suffering from violent toothache. I was in Italy...I had a perfect recollection of my waking life; I knew that I was sleeping and that my tooth was still aching. Yet I *did not feel it*...Next morning the pain was felt again and I had the tooth extracted. [Page 439.]

Van Eeden was aware that there was no muscular activity in dreams. As an experiment, he often sang, shouted and spoke loudly when lucid, but his wife assured him that throughout these behaviours he appeared to sleep peacefully.

He was keen to disagree with the old idea, stated by the German poet Novalis, that when we dream that we dream we are near waking. Van Eeden was adamant that lucid dreaming was associated with 'deep sleep' and that he only woke up from a lucid dream if he made a determined effort. He added that without exception all his lucid dreams had occurred in the hours between five and eight in the morning.

Perhaps reflecting van Eeden's moralistic character, he stated that he never noted anything sexual or erotic in his lucid dreams. They were generally of a blissful nature, and beautiful landscapes prevailed. For him, a lucid dream was often indicated a few days in advance, by experiencing flying in ordinary dreams. However, he could not accept the theory that the sensation of flying was caused by the rhythm of breathing, as Havelock Ellis believed.[4] Instead, van Eeden was of the opinion that the ease or not of flying and floating represented the general physical and psychological well-being of the dreamer. Difficulties in these behaviours were the result of a 'morbid condition of the body', or were symbolic of some current 'moral' problem.

In some experiments utilizing the lucid state, van Eeden attempted to 'call' persons—living or dead— and see if they would appear to him in his dream:

> I have called and seen several deceased persons in lucid dreams. I called and saw Myers (who coined the term 'telepathy') very shortly after his death, but it was not convincing and the atmosphere a little dismal. He seemed disappointed and sad. In July 1908, I called and saw him again, very distinctly and certainly this time...He tried to give me a password, but he could not, as if he were too weak. I have successfully called my father and different deceased friends and relations. [Page 453.]

Clearly, van Eeden was not greatly convinced that these were the genuine consciousnesses of those called, and he commented, 'Only hundreds of observations will bring an approach to certainty.'

Only one of his lucid dreams contained a prediction, and he ruefully described how it came true:

> In May 1903, I dreamed that I was in a little provincial Dutch town and at once encountered my brother-in-law, who had died some time before. I was absolutely sure it was he, and I knew that he was dead. He told me...that a financial catastrophe was impending for me. Somebody was going to rob me of 10,000 guilders... It came only too true, but the sum I lost was 20 times greater. At the time of the dream there seemed not to be the slightest probability of such a catastrophe. I was not even in possession of the money I lost afterwards. Yet it was the time when the first events took place—the railway strikes of 1903—that led to my financial ruin. [Page 451.]

Van Eeden recognized nine categories of dream in his own

experience: ordinary dreams, very vivid dreams, symbolic or 'mocking' dreams, general dream sensations, lucid dreams, demon dreams, wrong waking up dreams (i.e. false awakenings, see Chapter 8), initial dreams (at sleep onset), and pathological dreams (associated with fever and illness).

His reference to 'demons' controlling and appearing in some dreams is odd, but not unique. In fact, many people report seeing 'low creatures' in their dreams. Van Eeden would banish them by invoking God.

> These beings are always obscene and lascivious, and try to draw me into their acts and doings. They have no sex and appear alternately as a man, or a woman. Their aspect is very various and variable, changing every moment, taking all the fantastic forms that the old painters of the Middle Ages tried to reproduce, but with a certain weird plasticity and variability that no painting can express. [Page 455.]

He added:

> Whether these beings have a real existence or whether they are only creations of my fancy, to see them and to fight them takes away all their terror, all the uncanniness, the weirdness, of their tricks and pranks. [Page 456.]

Van Eeden's valuable comments on the dream state revealed the dream as a cleverly faked environment, where there were peculiar rules of physics and of cause and effect. Rarely were extraneous stimuli perceived within the condition, which was indubitably a true dream state. The inquisition of dream characters demonstrated how ingenious could be the process responsible for producing the dream's events.

Mary Arnold-Forster

Mrs Forster wrote on dreams in the early part of this century.[5] She sensed the potential of dreaming:

> I am sure that there are some simple secrets, some methods that can be learned, by means of which we may in some measure command dreams, and that, more than we yet realize, the control of our dreams lies within our power. [*Studies in Dreams*, page 52.]

She commented further:

> We shall only be able to enjoy the full value of our heritage in the
> dream world when we have discovered how to make full use of our
> powers of happy dreaming, and have learned to exercise at any rate
> a certain amount of selection and of control over the nature of our
> dreams. It is obvious that the advantages of such control would be
> great. [Page 52.]

While not technically a lucid dreamer, Mrs Forster made some
valuable comments on establishing dream control, in particular
from unpleasant situations. She described how she managed to
free herself from distressing dreams:

> I succeeded in starting an experiment in dream control. On various
> occasions long ago when a dream of grief or terror was becoming
> intolerably acute, the thought flashed into my sleeping mind, 'This
> is only a dream; if you wake, it will be over, and all will be well again.'
> I tried repeating this formula to myself from time to time, during the
> day and on going to bed, always in the same words—'Remember this
> is a dream. You are to dream no longer'—until, I suppose, the
> suggestion that I wanted to imprint upon the dream mind became
> more definite and more powerful than the impression of any dream.
> For a time after this secret had been fully learned, this would always
> waken me at once; nowadays, the formula having been said, I do not
> have to wake, though I may do so, but the original fear dream always
> ceases. It is simply switched off. [Page 57.]

A moment of lucidity, then, put the fearful situation into its
proper perspective, but Mrs Forster failed to utilize unpleasant
dream events as doorways to periods of full dream awareness.

'Oliver Fox' (Hugh G. Calloway)

Oliver Fox had many lucid dreams, which he termed 'dreams of
knowledge' or 'celestial dreams'. They could develop into 'out-of-
the-body' experiences or 'astral projections'. In his book *Astral
Projection*,[6] he pointed out that there were degrees of realization
and propounded a direct link between the dream's vividness and
level of awareness. Astral projection occurred, in him, if lucidity
was prolonged by effort. A 'click' was heard and he then found
himself in that subjectively different state. A second technique
concerning the dream state involved projecting himself from his
body when in a cataleptic state associated with a 'false awaken-

ing' (Chapter 8) following a lucid dream.

Fox related how, the night before an exam, he 'willed' himself in a lucid dream to see the exam paper. Actually, the two questions he saw did crop up as parts in the exam the next day!

In 1905, Fox argued with his girl-friend, Elsie, over his interest in the occult. He accused her of not knowing the meaning of astral projection. She declared that she could prove that she could also travel out of her body and would visit him that night. During the night, Fox had a false awakening in which he saw her emerge from a bluish-white cloud. The next day she excitedly told him how she had 'willed' herself to him. She stated six points about his room, which were all correct, including a ridge on a desk which Fox had not himself noticed. Elsie had never been to his room in real life. Unfortunately, Fox could not persuade her to make another astral visitation (pages 56–60).

Fox reported a little experiment concerning lucid dreaming that has become well known. He agreed to meet two friends, Slade and Elkington, in a dream one night on Southampton Common. Fox dreamed that he saw Elkington, but that Slade was absent. The next morning, Elkington said he had seen Fox, but that Slade was missing. Slade reported that he did not recall dreaming.

Probably, the experience can be put down to simple autosuggestion and expectation. Slade's absence could perhaps be explained by the fact that he may have previously said that he infrequently remembered dreaming. Nevertheless, the area is clearly fascinating and available for research by any lucid dreamers. It could be that the technique might facilitate psi communication.

Celia Green

Celia Green is the director of the Institute of Psychophysical Research, an institution established by her in 1961 at Oxford. She has written several seminal books, one of which, *Lucid Dreams*,[7] published in 1968, collated and analysed the few publications on lucid dreaming. This gathered and systematically examined material was presented in such a coherent and convincing manner that it was inevitably only a matter of time before proper scientific investigation of these dreams was initiated. It was the book that motivated this author to conduct the first sleep-laboratory studies into lucid dreams, and which resulted in many and varied discoveries.

Green compared the different reports from published writers, as well as those from four individual subjects known to her, and looked for consistencies—which were numerous. Questionnaire data was also included. Among the aspects of lucid dreams selected for consideration were: pre-lucidity; the initiation of lucidity; physical and psychological realism during lucidity; perceptual textures; memory of and in lucid dreaming; analytical thought; emotional qualities; dream-control; and ESP.

In a chapter entitled 'Experimental Prospects', Green pointed out that the first task facing experimental studies of lucid dreaming was to conduct sleep-laboratory studies to confirm that the lucid dream was a true REM dream. Realizing the importance of identifying the lucid dream in the polygraphic trace, she stated:

> ...This suggests the possibility that it might be possible to train subjects, lucidly dreaming during sleep, to exercise sufficient control over some, at least, of their motor functions to signal to the experimenter. [Page 130.]

As it turned out, that is precisely what was performed when I obtained the first signals from a lucid dreamer using eye-muscle communication, these muscles being unaffected by the general paralysis of dreaming sleep.

Patricia Garfield

This American psychologist wrote a useful book[8] which educated the reader in several different cultural backgrounds to dreaming, with the emphasis on developing dream lucidity, control and creativity. As an experienced recorder of dreams, Garfield gave some sensible advice on how to keep a dream diary. She pointed out that regular diary-keeping led to greatly increased dream recall.

Garfield urged that before sleep the individual should plan to remember whatever dreams happened, and place a pen and pad within easy reach. Even single fragments should be recorded. You should, on waking, lie still for a little while and allow the dream to stay in the mind. If nothing comes, you should run through a list of people in your life, and see if one of them triggers a dream memory. A physical change of position in bed might also bring to mind more memories. This recall should all be done with closed eyes. The first record, on paper or tape, should still be made with the eyes closed. Opening the eyes evaporates dream memories. The written accounts should be arranged into chronological order, for ease of following developments. Giving each dream a title identifies it and assists in subsequent recall. Eventually, 'translation' of dreams may be attempted. Garfield asserted that keeping a dream record can lead to greater self-understanding and help you increase your confidence and skills.

Garfield visited Malaysia and met with members of the Senoi tribe. These are a remarkably well-adjusted group who take great interest in their dreams, discuss them frequently, and encourage youngsters in the art of dreaming. Natural lucid dreaming is prevalent with these people.

Ann Faraday

In her book, *Dream Power*,[9] the sleep and dream researcher Ann Faraday reported having experienced a 'high lucid dream' which emerged from a lucid dream. In the 'high' state she felt tremendous exhilaration, as if under the influence of psychedelic drugs. She states, however, that the dream occurred before her experiments with drugs.

> ... the most extraordinary feeling came over me. Surges of energy pulsated throughout my body and I entered a 'high' in which I was completely transported on the kind of internal journey only those who have experienced psychedelic drugs would understand. I could actually feel my body being moved by this energy although I knew perfectly well that I was asleep. In the distance I could hear the hammering of the builders in the basement, a dog barking in a neighbour's garden, and the distant sound of traffic. I was filled with an enormous compassion for the whole of mankind for not being able to share my strange and wonderful experience at that moment. [Pages 294–5.]

Afterwards, she was able to enter a 'high' condition in a dream merely by wishing she had some LSD.

The early writers on lucid dreaming mentioned in this chapter were not known to many people. Therefore the whole concept of conscious, controllable dreaming had not yet crystallized in the public consciousness, and had no readily identifiable 'tag'. World-wide publicity, in the form of newspaper and magazine items, and radio and TV pieces, concerning the dream machine and signalling from within dreams, provided the first knowledge and interest in the field for many millions of people—as was reflected in my voluminous world-wide post!

Having comprehended the notion, many people will have recalled, perhaps vaguely, some personal episode of lucidity or pre-lucidity from years ago. More importantly, the information will have 'set the scene' psychologically, so that when a pre-lucid condition arises in the future, the thought 'This is a conscious, controllable, i.e. "lucid", dream', will spring to mind. At that moment, the full significance and potential of the situation will be realized by the dreamer and not lost, as would probably otherwise have been the case.

It is guaranteed to happen that within a week or two after I have given a talk on lucid dreaming—say at a university, seminar weekend, or some society—I get feedback from people in the audience who had not heard of the topic before the talk but who had now actually experienced their first exciting lucid dream. That point emphasizes the great consequence of putting adequate labelling on phenomena and, parenthetically, makes one pause to wonder what wealth of other, as yet unknown, experiences might exist.

As things turned out, in man's striving towards an understanding of dreaming, the phenomenon of lucid dreaming had, unfortunately, been very considerably under-reported. This affected theoretical thinking adversely. It has become abundantly clear now that the investigation of lucid dreams is the royal road to a knowledge of dreaming generally. Moreover, the findings from such research can provide tangible facts and consistencies on which to hang theories—a considerable improvement over the procession of unprovable 'theories' that were presented in the past.

References

1. Saint-Denys, Hervey de (1982; orig. 1867) *Dreams and How to Guide Them*, trans. Nicholas Fry, ed. M. Schatzman. Duckworth, London.
2. Van Eeden, F. (1913) A study of dreams. *Proceedings of the Society for Psychical Research*, **XXVI** (Pt. LXVII), 431–61.

3. Mach, E. (1954) *The Analysis of Sensations*. Dover, New York.
4. Ellis, H. (1931) *The World of Dreams*. Constable & Co Ltd., London.
5. Arnold-Forster, Mary (1921) *Studies in Dreams*. Allen & Unwin, London.
6. Fox, O. (1962) *Astral Projection*. University Books, Inc., New York.
7. Green, C. (1968) *Lucid Dreams*. Institute of Psychophysical Research, Oxford.
8. Garfield, Patricia (1974) *Creative Dreaming*. Ballantine Books, New York.
9. Faraday, Ann (1972) *Dream Power*. Hodder & Stoughton, London.

4

Further findings

Apart from sleep-lab studies of lucid dreaming, valuable as they are, there are other ways of finding out general characteristics of these dreams, or of utilizing them for useful research.

One simple technique is to collate questionnaire information gathered from a large number of people who report having lucid dreams. One British national newspaper (the *Sunday People*) actually printed a questionnaire for me in an article on my work, and hundreds of helpful people responded, providing much original and fascinating data.

A particularly useful method of exploring the internal features of lucid dreams is to instruct subjects to perform specific set tasks when lucid and report back. Naturally, subjects are not told what to expect when they respond in isolation—not having conferred with other subjects—so as not to bias the results. These approaches have revealed some extremely interesting facts about lucid dreams.

The 'light-switch' effect[1]

The discovery of this consistent phenomenon in dreams arose because in listening to and reading many dream reports I noticed that the inability of the dreamer to switch on a light in the dream scenery cropped up repeatedly. It was not an effect that would ever have been anticipated by any previous dream theory, so was certainly not sought in the past.

Having the suspicion that such a phenomenon existed in dreams, it had to be shown to be present, scientifically. It took no effort to realize that habitual lucid dreamers were the ideal people to confirm or disprove the hypothesis. The experiment was simple. Eight lucid dreamers in different parts of the country were simply requested to perform the task of turning on an electric light switch in the dream scenery when next lucid, and to report in detail what happened. There were no indications of my own expectations in the instructions.

The subjects reported thus:

1 'I went to the bedroom light switch and turned it on. To my surprise, a light came on behind me in a room to the side, but not in the bedroom. Then I tried the kitchen light switch. Nothing happened. Quite annoyed and frustrated that I couldn't get the lights to turn on, I went back to the bedroom and said to the young man, "What's with the lights? They won't turn on!"'

2 'I switched it on and off several times and looked up at the light, which was a naked bulb. It kept sparking and flickering—I could see the filament glow orangey-red. I thought "Typical of this place, nothing works properly."'

3 'I just couldn't find the switch and seemed to search for ages.'

4 'Attempting to switch on the (dream) bedside light is fruitless as the bulb will not come on.'

5 'I tried to switch the light on—it would not come on.'

6 'I tried switching on the lights in the corridor, but nothing happened.'

7 'I know I'm dreaming when the bedside lamp will not switch on.'

8 'I covered my eyes. I felt myself touch my eyelids and I couldn't see. I then felt the light switch and everything became very bright.'

Now in the last mentioned account it looks as if the light came on with no difficulty, but it is necessary to know that immediately beforehand the subject had switched the light off. That additional piece of information gives a clue to what may well be happening in the situation. It seems that there exists a 'ceiling limit' on 'brightness' in the dream imagery at any one point in the dream. This maximum level varies over time, for we know that some dreams are very bright and some may be very dark. If the dreamer, using techniques of dream control, attempts to violate that (presumably) physiologically set ceiling, the dream-producing process has to rationalize what is going on by avoiding any activity in the dream that would result in an increase in brightness. Thus, the light switches can't be found, the light is fused, and so on. The dream is fooling the dreamer.

This is a very interesting observation, because it suggests that an autonomous process operates producing dreams. It is not a free-ranging process, because it has to function within such limitations of imagery. Other less plausible explanations are that the effect represents a sleep-maintaining process which avoids dream scenes where a light suddenly switches on, since in waking life that is associated with rousing, or that the pheno-menon may symbolically allude to the 'lack of energy' of the sleep state—but its apparent specificity does not support that point.

There are some points in dreams where brightness does suddenly increase, naturally. It can by hypothesized that those moments will be directly linked to random bursts of stimulation that occur in the brain from time to time in REM sleep and cause the REMs.

The light-switch effect was the first universal phenomenon to be shown in dreams. Other researchers have confirmed its exist-ence,[2, 3] and it is expected that the phenomenon will feature much in all future discussions concerning dream-production processes.

There are other apparent universal features that are being discovered.[4] Anomalies appear with many electrical appliances in dreams, as if the dream simply cannot suddenly perform certain tasks to order. For instance:

I went over to the van, climbed into the driver's seat and turned the ignition key. There was no sound at all from the engine, and I heard myself sing.

I turn on the radio and then sit down. I am singing away, but there is no music coming out of the radio.

I turned the keys and the engine fired. I put the wipers on, but could not persuade the car to move although the engine was quietly running. The lights did not work.

There is often a lack of co-ordination between the different imaging modalities (i.e. visual, auditory, etc). Perhaps they are following rather independent pathways in the dream, and one form may have priority of effect over others at any one time. Physiological factors may be important in that each modality may require neuronal stimulation (say, from the same source that generates REMs) but that this stimulation may not be equally distributed, hence the lack of synchronization. Possibly, the modalities are so loosely linked that completely separate dreams may be experienced simultaneously by the different forms.

The significance of such consistencies must not be underestimated. Once a reliable effect can be demonstrated, then it acts as a fixed element which has to be explained by subsequent theories. Hypotheses have to be formulated and tested by experiments. This is a wonderful time of discovery in dreams, and offers a tremendous opportunity for theorists to tackle these new findings.

Scene-shifts

Another familiar effect that I came across frequently in dream reports was that of a spontaneous scene-shift happening when the (dream) eyes were covered or closed. This was another task subsequently given to habitual lucid dreamers to perform and report back.[5] Six persons, all female, gave their findings:

1   I looked up at the sky and blinked. I then appeared to be baby-sitting at a place where the man was Joss Ackland, the actor. Later, I looked at a bright light and shut my eyes. This time, I appeared in a big house with a massive winding staircase. I blinked again and was transported to the present.

2   I put my arm over my eyes to protect me from the fire, and found myself outside the house.

3   I have tried to perform this experiment several times. Each time the surroundings seemed to change, or the dream fade away.

4   The sun came through and I saw a monolith—white and tall against the blue sky. I closed my eyes in relief, but when I opened them I was in a lift on the top floor and my carrier bag had changed to a suit-case.

5 I see some children who are caged. As I walk by, most
ignore me but some run along the side of their cages and
shout abuse and fling themselves against the bars, spitting
and snarling. Their eyes narrow with hate and their milk-
white teeth are sharp. I close my eyes. It is hard to do so.
There is blackness, then the dream is re-run.

6 I looked towards the sun. When I opened my eyes, I
couldn't see anything but I could hear people talking and
the waves on the beach. I tried to walk but seemed to be
fixed to the spot.

The results confirmed, then, that something drastic happens
when the dream is interrupted by the simple expedient of
covering the eyes. There is, of course, no physical closing of the
eyes—which are in fact already closed—so the effect is a purely
mental one. Definite changes of scene were reported in the first
four cases. The dream re-ran in case 5, which involved in fact a
scene-change back to the beginning. In case 6, sleep paralysis
was experienced, indicating perhaps partial waking. We can
conclude that this method of scene-shifting is an effective and
instantaneous technique in dream control.

A study of what precisely happens at such scene-shifts will
provide meaningful and essential information in the attempt to
comprehend dreaming. It has become obvious that there are
associations between the 'before' and 'after' pictures at a scene-
change. Data is currently being accumulated on this important
topic. Thus, for instance, one lucid dreamer reported:

'Before' scene:

A street with a wall at the end having a central gateway; a shop
window on either side of the street, with a mannequin in one
window; a chair, prominent in the other shop window.

'After' scene:

A scene inside a café, with a male server at a hatchway, and seats in
the foreground.

The subject provided detailed drawings of both pictures. The
gateway—the main feature in the first picture—seems to have
become the hatchway in the second. There is just one figure
(mannequin/man) in each scene. The second scene has several
basic similarities with the first.

This is crucial evidence and indicates that the dream progresses via visually close pathways.

Actually, I had already discovered such a scene-shift effect several years earlier in some research into 'hypnotic' dreams.[6, 7] I had devised a special and original method of externalizing the imagery of these dreams. I used 'deep trance' hypnosis subjects and got them to have a dream on a stated topic. The dream would be permitted to run for a very short while and would be stopped on a signal. The subject was then instructed to project the scene onto a drawing-board and trace round the outlines, at the same time describing colours and textures for later filling-in. The dream would be started and stopped many times so that, after several hours, a sequence of pictures from the dream was obtained. In amongst all this fascinating material was a patently clear scene-change phenomenon.

For instance, one subject produced a 'before' picture consisting of a bird's-eye view of a living room, with three people present, and three items of furniture. The very next picture showed a schoolroom, seen from a slightly lower angle, but with a teacher and two pupils present, and also three items of furniture. The colour blue predominates in both pictures (Fig. 9a).

Another subject traced a scene displaying a green snake wrapped round a tree. The next picture revealed a curved green pipe emerging from a brown brick wall (Fig. 9b).

It should be stated that I do not now accept that the results were due to 'hypnosis'. I have become extremely sceptical about that alleged state. I believe that the subjects all had good visual imaging abilities and the 'hypnosis' was not at all necessary.

What seemed to be happening was that pictorial elements from the first picture were rearranged so that they constituted a new scene. To the subject, the scene was completely transformed but, on inspection, the common features were plain. It was as if the dream was following some law of least effort and making what use it could of the material available.

On reflection, there is no reason to think that some separate dream-producing process should be employed in nocturnal dreams as against 'hypnotic' dreams, so we can assume that we are dealing here with the same basic phenomenon. It can therefore be predicted with confidence that similar findings will result from studies using good visualizers in the waking state.

(a) Person 1

A bird's eye view of a living-room with three people and three items of furniture, which changes to a classroom with a teacher, two children and three items of furniture. Blue predominates in both pictures

(b) Person 2

A green snake wrapped round a tree changes to a green pipe emerging from a brown-brick wall

Fig. 9.
Scene-shift phenomena in 'hypnotic' dreams. The pictures have been 'externalized' by getting the subject to stop the dream, project the scene onto a drawing-board, and then trace the picture

Causes of lucidity

What sorts of situations in ordinary dreams appear to cause the sudden entrance of consciousness, so transforming the experience into lucid dreaming? No systematic study had been conducted into this highly relevant area, but a marvellous opportunity for collecting much data on lucid dreams arose in 1980 when the *Sunday People* published an article on my work and included a questionnaire for readers.[8] In addition, readers were asked to send in a report of one lucid dream.

Some 500 readers, who had frequent lucid dreams, responded. One hundred of the accounts were randomly selected for analysis.[9] The largest category was that of some *inconsistency* causing the awareness of dreaming. This could be broken down into the following:

(a) **IP**   A *person* (or persons) in the dream triggers lucidity in some way, e.g. appearance, behaviour, voice, etc.   16%

(b) **IO**   Specific *objects*, or animals, cause lucidity. This sub-group included seeing faces suddenly that then vanish.   14%

(c) **IS**   Something odd is noticed about *self*, e.g. body, circumstances, driving car when can't in reality, etc.   6%

(d) **ISI**   *Scenery* (*inside* a building) is observed to be wrong in some way.   5%

(e) **ISO**   *Scenery* (*outside*) is seen to be wrong in some way.   5%

(f) **IM**   *Malfunctions* of equipment cause suspicion of dreaming.   3%

(g) **IH**   *Home* or residence from previous period of life is recognized.   2%

(h) **ID**   Seeing persons who are known to be *dead* in reality.   2%

$$\underline{\text{TOTAL} = 53\%}$$

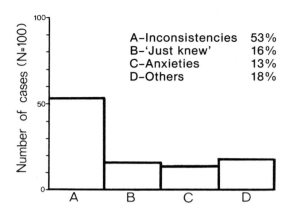

Fig. 10.
Apparent causes of lucidity in dreams

The next largest main category was where the dreamer 'just knew' they were dreaming. No noticeable cause could be cited.

TOTAL = 16%

Anxieties constitute the third main category:

(a) AH Threat, attack or pursuit by a person or persons (*human*). 6%

(b) AP Dreamer anxious about a *phobic* situation, e.g. if dreamer has fear of heights. 2%

(c) AU Other *unpleasant* situations, e.g. funeral, death, accident. 2%

(d) AL Dreamer has *lost* something or someone. 2%

(e) AA *Animal* threat, attack or pursuit. 1%

TOTAL = 13%

The remaining apparent causes of lucidity were:

(a) R *Recurring* dream recognized. 9%

(b) U *Unclear* how dreamer became lucid from the report. 9%

TOTAL = 18%

Settings at lucidity

The 100 sample lucid dreams were also analysed to determine the setting at the moment of onset of lucidity. There were three main categories: Inside; Outside; Ambiguous. In addition, another dimension was: Familiar; Unfamiliar; Questionable; Distorted; Geographical. In some accounts, no setting was mentioned. Two judges independently rated each account, and there was 89 per cent agreement between the judges.

The break-down was:

	%
OU (Outside, Unfamiliar) e.g. 'cave'	23%
OQ (Outside, Questionable) e.g. 'on a gondola'	12%
OF (Outside, Familiar) e.g. 'outside Linda's house'	9%
OD (Outside, Distorted) e.g. 'distorted garden'	4%
OG (Outside, Geographical) e.g. 'middle of the ocean'	2%
IU (Inside, Unfamiliar) e.g. 'inside a small three-bedroomed house'	5%
IQ (Inside, Questionable) e.g. 'on the floor'	6%
IF (Inside, Familiar) e.g. 'in the kitchen'	17%
ID (Inside, Distorted) e.g. 'school stairs'	6%
AU (Ambiguous, Unfamiliar) e.g. 'an old school'	1%
AQ (Ambiguous, Questionable) e.g. 'on my way back home'	3%
NS (No setting stated)	12%

So, the most frequent setting category at lucidity was a place outside, which was unfamiliar to the dreamer.

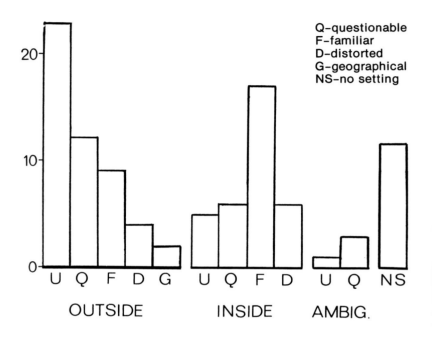

Fig. 11.
Settings-at-lucidity frequencies

Results of the newspaper questionnaire

The information from the returned questionnaire of 365 lucid dreamers, as a consequence of the *Sunday People* item, was collated and gave much basic group-data on these dreams and the experiencers. Of the respondents, 271 were female, 82 male, and 12 gave no gender. Most were aged between 20 and 40, and the mean age was 32 years.

Lucid dreamers reading this book may like to compare their own experiences with this mass-data:

1 How often do you experience a lucid dream? %

(a) One per year on average	26	7.1
(b) Two per year on average	50	13.7
(c) One per month on average	72	19.7
(d) Two per month on average	60	16.4
(e) Four per month on average	60	16.4
(f) Two plus per week on average	89	24.4
(g) No response	8	2.2

2 Do they tend to occur in batches?

(a) Yes	121	33.1
(b) No	231	63.3
(c) No response	13	3.6

3 How do lucid dream pictures compare with ordinary dream pictures?

(a) Less vivid	22	6.0
(b) Same	108	29.6
(c) More vivid	229	62.7
(d) No response	6	1.6

4 What is your reaction to finding yourself in a lucid dream?

(a) Pleasant	117	32.0
(b) Neutral	79	21.6
(c) Unpleasant	131	35.9
(d) No response	38	10.4

5 At what time do lucid dreams tend to occur?

(a) Up to 2 a.m.	21	5.8
(b) 2–5 a.m.	165	45.2
(c) 5 a.m. onwards	109	29.9
(d) No response/do not know	70	19.2

6 How long do you think your lucid
dreams last on average?

(a)	Seconds	36	9.9
(b)	Up to 5 minutes	66	18.1
(c)	Up to 10 minutes	69	18.9
(d)	Up to 15 minutes	59	16.2
(e)	Up to 30 minutes	54	14.8
(f)	More than 30 minutes	55	15.1
(g)	No response	26	7.1

7 How does your thinking in lucid dreams
compare with that when you are awake?

(a)	More clear	165	45.2
(b)	Same	136	37.3
(c)	Less clear	57	15.6
(d)	No response	6	1.6

8 Have you performed experiments in lucid
dreams?

(a)	Yes	111	30.4
(b)	No	241	66.0
(c)	No response	13	3.6

9 Have you ever 'flown' (by flapping your
arms) in a lucid dream?

(a)	Yes	164	44.9
(b)	No	192	53.6
(c)	No response	8	2.2

10 How do colours appear in lucid dreams
compared with real life?

(a)	Brighter	106	29.0
(b)	Same	148	40.5
(c)	Duller	47	12.9
(d)	No colour	48	13.2
(e)	No response	16	4.4

11 How do colours appear in ordinary
dreams compared with real life?

(a) Brighter	59	16.2
(b) Same	158	43.3
(c) Duller	72	19.7
(d) No colour	58	15.9
(e) No response	18	4.9

12 Do things in lucid dreams ever appear to be distorted?

(a) Yes	108	29.6
(b) No	219	60.0
(c) Don't know	29	7.9
(d) No response	9	2.5

13 How does time seem to pass in lucid dreams?

(a) More slowly than in real life	77	21.0
(b) Same	103	28.2
(c) Faster	92	25.2
(d) Timeless	75	20.5
(e) No response	18	4.9

14 Can you control the course of events in lucid dreams?

(a) Very easily	38	10.4
(b) Fairly easily	85	23.3
(c) With difficulty	84	23.0
(d) No control possible	61	16.7
(e) Have not tried to control	87	23.8
(f) No response	10	2.7

15 Do you usually wake up after a lucid dream?

(a) Yes	311	85.2
(b) No	49	13.4
(c) No response	5	1.4

16 Have you ever thought you had woken from a lucid dream only to discover later that you were still dreaming?

(a)	Yes	252	69.0
(b)	No	109	29.9
(c)	No response	4	1.1

17 How memorable are lucid dreams compared with ordinary dreams?

(a)	More	285	78.1
(b)	Same	68	18.6
(c)	Less	9	2.4
(d)	No response	3	0.8

18 What other senses do you experience in lucid dreams apart from sight?

(a)	Hearing	275	75.3
(b)	Taste	76	20.8
(c)	Smell	96	26.3
(d)	Touch	257	70.4
(e)	Pain	177	48.5

19 Have you experienced strong emotions in lucid dreams?

(a)	Yes	319	87.4
(b)	No	40	10.9
(c)	No response	6	1.6

Comments

While most people have not, or have only very rarely, experienced a natural lucid dream, the questionnaire data illustrate that some individuals are very familiar with them. In fact, a quarter of the sample had them two or more times a week. There is clearly a considerable divide between someone who never recalls a dream and a person who manipulates and enjoys a dream experience every night. Surely, the non-recaller suffers profound experiential deprivation!

The question on lucid dreams coming in 'batches' was included because some dreamers had reported that this is how they seemed to come, but the data show that most dreamers did not notice any such thing.

The quality of the lucid dream in relation to other (ordinary) dreams and to waking life was found to be different in some interesting ways. Pictorial vividness was greater than in ordinary dreams in two-thirds of the sample. Exaggerated colours were noted more in lucid dreams than in ordinary dreams. However, the presence of consciousness in lucid dreams may assist such observations whereas they might be ignored in the usual dreams because of their less observant nature. I have noticed a perspective distortion in my own lucid dreams, but only 30 per cent of the respondents reported visual distortion.

The finding that 45 per cent of the sample said their lucid dreams arose between 2 and 5 a.m. was somewhat surprising. Lucid dreamers I had studied stated that they tended to appear in later REM periods. Essentially, though, they are indeed a phenomenon of the second half of the night.

The perception of the passage of time during lucidity was shown to vary greatly between subjects. Roughly equal proportions thought that time passed slower, was the same, or was faster than in waking life. A similar number considered that time seemed static.

The oft-reported crystal-clear thinking of the lucid state was picked up in the data. Nearly half the subjects said their thinking was even more clear than when awake! This, presumably, is linked to the elevated level of brain activity in REM sleep.

That lucid dreams have a great psychological effect on the dreamer was reflected in the finding that 78 per cent of subjects said that these dreams were more memorable than ordinary ones. Feelings can be released in lucid dreams, including full sexual orgasm, and 87 per cent stated that they had experienced strong emotions during lucidity.

Dreams are predominantly visual, but the other senses are also present. Taste was the least registered sensation, close to smell, but hearing and touch were strongly reported.

It can be assumed that before the newspaper article appeared virtually none of the respondents had ever heard of a lucid dream although they experienced the phenomenon. A quarter of the sample had never tried to control their lucid dreams, two-thirds of the sample had not tried to experiment, and about a half had not attempted to 'fly', so an understanding of the potential of the state was lacking, perhaps, in many subjects. It is conceivably for that reason that about a third of the respondents reported an unpleasant reaction to finding themselves lucid. Knowledge of the great possibilities available in the condition could readily alter such an attitude.

Contents

The analysis of modern, natural lucid-dream reports from 'naive' subjects reveals some interesting, amusing and touching features.

Lucidity and sex

Sexual activity is quite often referred to in lucid dream accounts. It is probably under-reported because the topic is delicate to some dreamers. Several lucid dreamers have told me that on becoming lucid they deliberately engineer sexual situations using dream control techniques.

There are, as always, individual differences—so the degree of sexual involvement in the dream varies between subjects.

Some people enter into full sexual relationships with dream characters who are strangers:

> I went for a walk within my old school as I remembered it. A tennis teacher asked me to wait, as I passed the courts. She ran up to me and kissed me. I was certain that this, being too good to be true, would waken me—but it did not. She was wearing a white skirt and singlet, with white socks and plimsolls. She pulled me down on top of her onto the grass. I remember that people were walking past and took no notice of us and tennis continued on the adjacent courts. I took down her pants, and she unzipped me. She opened her legs and we made love. I even orgasmed with her, in full, and felt an ejaculation inside her. At this point I awoke.
>
> It was a complete, yet very sad dream—because it was a very beautiful experience and I knew I could never know who she was nor see her again. She was so very real. Incidentally, I did not have a 'wet' dream—though the sensation was real enough.

That final point illustrates the highly cerebral nature of sex in humans.

The next dreamer found herself having sex with a pop-star whom she greatly admired:

> The dream involved making love with someone I do find attractive

and very sexy, and think about quite often. I could actually touch the person's skin and feel the softness of the skin—also, the actual sexual act. I have never experienced this type of dream before and feel really embarrassed. My dreams are usually about friends or my career. I knew I was dreaming throughout, because the guy involved was Sting from the group 'Police'.

The realization of dreaming permits some dreamers to indulge in behaviour with people they know, that would not normally happen because of prohibitive circumstances:

I was with an old lover who has in waking life left my life completely. We were making love when I realized this was impossible as he had gone. I chided myself for being so childish as to even dream up things I couldn't have. After I'd accepted I was dreaming, I realized I'd been enjoying myself and let my lover carry on.

I have experienced strong emotions in my lucid dreams. I recently had a dream in which I had a passionate sexual affair with my brother-in-law. I knew all the time I was dreaming, but everything was so real. I could feel him as though he were there, and could even smell his after-shave.

I experiment sexually in my lucid dreams. I am a girl of 17 and have not had sex yet with a boy in waking life, but my boy-friend appears in my lucid dreams and he makes love to me very passionately and it is very enjoyable.

Most ordinary dreams are totally forgotten. However, while using the dream machine, some sexual situations in dreams cause the device to trigger—when it is used in the 'nightmare' mode—so bringing waking awareness to what was just transpiring.

I was using the dream machine in the mode where it wakens you immediately a pre-determined value is reached. I was woken from a very sexual dream in which I had been caressing a woman's breasts and she had responded by squeezing my penis for a long time. The dream was very vivid and I continued to feel the stimulation for some minutes after I woke. I would not have known I ever had the dream if the device had not woken me.

Seeing the dead

The awareness of dreaming may be triggered by seeing someone in a dream who is known to be dead. At the same time, the clarity and verisimilitude of the encounter may cause a strong emotional reaction. Such a meeting can be one of the most moving experiences that can happen to a dreamer:

> I saw my father in a lucid dream. In real life he had been terribly crippled and in pain. He had been very ill and became progressively more pathetic over several years. I knew it was a dream—and it was extremely bright, clear and vivid. My father was fully restored to health. He could walk, move normally, and looked happy and healthy. 'Look,' he said, 'I'm all right now.' I was so very happy to see him like that, that I cried copiously in the dream and upon waking.

Heaven-like scenes are occasionally viewed in lucid dreams, and may have a profound effect on the dreamer:

> I walked along a path on a mountain-side. The green of new grass, young trees, colours of the lovely flowers, were unbelievably bright. The stream at the foot of the mountain sparkled like diamonds. The sun shone golden through the trees onto the path and one broad beam, further along, shone brightest of all. I thought, 'When I reach that, I will look right up into heaven.' When I nearly reached it, two men in fine white robes came towards me, carrying golden crooks and wearing golden sandals. One of them came towards me, and I knelt down, and then woke up. Never again was I unhappy about where my late husband was. I now knew.

Daredevils

The lucid state is ideal for some dreamers to try daredevil acts, safe in the knowledge that no 'comeback' will ensue and no harm will occur:

> I thought to myself, 'I'm in a dream, so why not make the best of it?' So as I was dreaming, I decided to do something stupid. I got off the bus I was on and as it was hot I took off my clothes and ran along the street to see how people stared at me. You see, I didn't care because I knew I was dreaming and it seemed fun.

> I dreamed that I went to the toilet. I got up and walked out to the landing on my way there, but the light switch did not work. I knew from previous occasions that this was indicative of a lucid dream. This was definitely confirmed by other tests. I decided to do

something exciting, so I went to the top of the stairs and did a big leap into the air. I floated down slowly, with a feeling of exhilaration.

Flying

One of the most pleasurable activities for the lucid dreamer is flying. Techniques include flapping the arms like a bird, zooming around like a rocket, or simply floating along. It's something we simply cannot do in waking existence, yet it is effortless and natural in the dream world. When the level of imagery is bright and vivid, the aerial views can be spectacular and the feeling of mastery is beyond compare.

I had a dream in which I was by a massive bridge over a river. I wanted to fly up to it, so I put out my arms and took off. I was fully aware that I was dreaming. Everything was remarkably vivid. I looked down and saw cars and people on the bridge. I swept up to the highest parts and saw the structure close to in great detail. The clarity was marvellous and the colours fantastic. In the distance I could see fields and roads. The water rippled realistically. I had a breathless sense of excitement and felt like Superman!

I have flown, or rather soared at great heights, viewing scenes and areas of the world I have not seen, but have read about or perhaps viewed on TV. In my dreams I am able to float down to any place I choose. I am always dressed in a white dress-type apparel which is of a cloudy appearance. My arms do not flap but are able to move about quite naturally whilst I am in the air. To leave the ground, my arms are always extended, above my head, with the palms of my hands touching.

I was floating up what seemed a never-ending bright green hill, dressed in long rainbow-coloured clothes, barefoot, with flowing hair. It was a warm day and it seemed as if everywhere was filled with warm yellow sunshine. I saw a rider on horseback on the hilltop. He saw me and rode down. As he came closer, he pulled on the horse's reins and the horse reared on its back legs (like in the films). I saw that the rider was handsome with a compelling face. He looked like a cross between a gipsy and a pirate and was dressed in a red satin shirt with a bandana round his head, and had brilliant blue trousers. He looked very proud and regal. He smiled, and in his eyes and smile it seemed that I had found eternal peace, joy, tranquillity and love. I realized that I was a peasant maiden as I was dressed in clothes of years ago. It was a very intensely emotional and beautiful dream, and I knew throughout that it was a dream.

Experimenters

Habitual lucid dreamers tend to explore the characteristics of the dream state and often encounter interesting effects:

> I realized the absurdity of using a pedestrian crossing in a dream when I was not in a material form. Presumably, as I was not solid, a vehicle could pass harmlessly through the space which I was occupying, or I could pass through the vehicle. I decided to test this idea in the most extreme way I could think of, which was to attempt to travel through someone else in the dream. I selected a passer-by at random and, moving horizontally, aimed myself at a point just beneath the ribs. My experience was entirely unexpected: on entry, vision stopped, but I felt with a fairly life-like intensity sensations of warmth and moisture. These lasted only a second or two, then I emerged the other side of the body.

> In one lucid dream, I visited someone (a friend). I knew it was a dream. When I related the story to my friend and told him what I had seen and the rough time, he was very surprised as what I had told him was actually happening at that time.

> I found myself in a lucid dream. I encountered a weird shape which acted like a tiger. It had yellow and brown markings, but I knew I was dreaming and I tried an experiment. I stared at the shape, which twisted and turned, then lay still on the floor. It was a raffia shopping-bag—the same colour as the 'tiger shape'.

> When I become aware that I am dreaming, I try to do silly things to see if I can make them happen, like flying and walking through walls. Once, when I was 15, I even managed to beat up a school bully. There was a lot of satisfaction in that.

> During my experimentation I found that a certain level of will-power was needed to produce results, but excitement has a negative effect. Dropping the pressure (will-power and/or excitement) seems to enhance the results as well. Therefore, the very ingredients that can produce lucid dreams at will can also stop them or cut them short. The trick seems to be to control emotions at all levels.

Sometimes I look at my watch in a lucid dream—obviously my 'dream' watch. It is usually accurate to within two to three minutes. I know this because I normally wake up soon afterwards and check the time.

Meeting the famous

Not infrequently lucid dreamers meet famous people in their dreams:

> I won the film star Roger Moore in a raffle in a lucid dream. I was embarrassed because I didn't know what to do with him and I just felt he would think it was all a drag. I have been to many places with the Queen in my lucid dreams, and the Queen Mother has shown me all around Balmoral!

Stimulus intrusion retardation effect

If a dream is in full flow, but some strong, alerting, external (or perhaps internal) stimulus penetrates the dream, I have observed a marked slowing of the dream's current activities. The effect has also been reported by other subjects. This 'grinding to a halt' is of some theoretical importance because it produces a further fact for the gaining of insight into the dream-producing process.

At such a point, the visual imagery continues at the same 'brightness', but its rate of production decreases considerably. An example that I can give is of a dream where I was busily driving along a road. The car seemed to stop dead. The picture 'froze' and the sound imagery disappeared. The external sound source was then perceived, and I awoke.

The phenomenon probably has a survival value, in that the external stimulus could be the sensed approach of a predator, so the dream must be interrupted somehow. The theoretical significance is that the level of visual imagery does not diminish, but that the rate does. This suggests that the internal perception of visual imagery is unstoppable in REM sleep. The internal 'eyes' cannot be 'closed', and the 'TV screen' cannot be 'switched off'. Only the flow of material from the 'video player' can be interrupted. Possibly, the amount of slowing may be related to the psychological significance of the stimulus. Auditory imagery is different in that it ceases immediately.

This information indicates that two distinct processes are involved in the visual part of dream production. The first is concerned with the quality of imagery—'brightness', 'colour', etc. (and involves the 'light-switch' phenomenon). The second deals with the dream material and its rate of display—the 'film' or 'video tape'. This retardation effect needs to be studied experimentally.

Discussion

Some powerful new means are clearly at hand to crack the secrets of dreams. In particular, the simple expedient of instructing lucid dreamers to carry out various experiments while lucid and report back is yielding considerable returns. While with ordinary dreams consistent effects would be very difficult to notice, and are perhaps completely overlooked in dream reports, the special state of lucidity makes insightful observation straightforward and efficient. Subjects do not have to be skilled introspectionists; they just perform the required tasks and state what happened. In fact it is preferable that subjects know little about what has been written about lucidity, since any element of expectation could perhaps tend to affect the subject's perceptions—as happens in any observation in waking life too.

Such lucidity research is in a wide open scientific field awaiting full discovery. Some important data could be acquired without the necessity of lucidity. For instance, the several phenomena of scene-shifts could be studied even without dreams, by using awake subjects who possess good visualizing powers. The processes concerned could reasonably be applied to dreaming. This is a time of gathering essential data by experimentation. The correct scientific procedure is first to collect facts and then to fit a theory, which must be constantly modified until it corresponds with those facts. Unfortunately, the wide range of dream theories up to now has been based on much supposition and conjecture, but few facts.

There is much to busy sleep and dream researchers for many years to come, using the new techniques of signalling from within lucid dreams and getting subjects to perform 'internal study' experiments. Already, we have learned more about dreaming in the past 10 years or so than in all the preceding millennia.

References

1. Hearne, K.M.T. (1981) A 'light-switch phenomeon' in lucid dreams. *Journal of Mental Imagery*, 5 (2), 97–100.
2. Tholey, P. (1983) Techniques for inducing and manipulating lucid dreams. *Perceptual and Motor Skills*, 57, Part 1, 79–90.
3. Blackmore, S. Personal communication.
4. Hearne, K.M.T. (1982) Effects of performing certain set tasks in the lucid dream state. *Perceptual and Motor Skills*, 54, 259–62.
5. *Ibid.*
6. Hearne, K.M.T. (1973) Some investigations into hypnotic dreams using a new technique. B.Sc. Thesis, University of Reading.
7. Hearne, K.M.T. (1987) A new perspective in dream imagery. *Journal of Mental Imagery*, 11 (2), 75–82.
8. Jeffrey, B. (1980) Look inside your dream machine. *Sunday People*, 21 September, 16–17.
9. Hearne, K.M.T. (1983) Features of lucid dreams: questionnaire data and content analyses. *Journal of Lucid Dream Research*, 1 (1), 3–20.

5

The Dream Machine and Lucidity

Normally, as was seen in the last chapter, spontaneous lucidity arises from noticing some incongruity in the dream scenery. My idea was that if a standard signal could be incorporated into an ordinary dream, at such a level that waking would not occur, then it might be recognized by the dreamer as a 'cue' for lucidity. After considerable research, the method selected involved giving slight electric shocks, which feel like pin pricks, to the wrist. It was a convenient technique, easily controlled by a microprocessor system.

A proper study, using sleep-laboratory monitoring of subjects, was conducted using the new method. Twelve female subjects, mostly students, were used in the tests. They were between 19 and 33 years of age, and the average was 24 years. Each person spent only one night in the sleep-laboratory, so any successes would be particularly noteworthy. Before subjects went to sleep they were told all about lucid dreaming and the purpose of the experiment was fully described. Then the following instructions were given:

> During the night, when you are asleep and dreaming, you will receive four electrical impulses to the wrist. They are meant to make you realize that you are dreaming, that is, to make you become 'lucid'. Think of each pulse as being a word in this sentence: THIS IS A DREAM. When you have felt the shocks, wait a few seconds and observe the dream scenery, then signal that you are aware that you are dreaming by making a few regularly spaced left–right eye movements. You will be woken shortly afterwards and asked to describe what happened.

A short period of practice then ensued, in which pulses were sent to the subject and the eye-signal responses were tried. The lights were switched off in the sleep-lab bedroom.

The subjects were wired up for conventional sleep monitoring but two extra electrodes were placed on the wrist for the purpose of electrical stimulation. The level of shocks was such that it was quite acceptable to the subject.

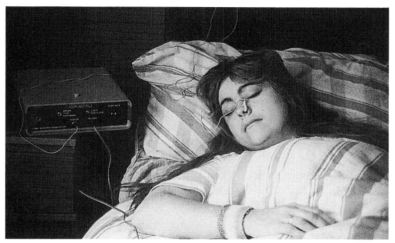

Fig. 12.
Subject wired up to dream machine for lucidity induction

Unknown to the participants, a 'catch-trial' was included in the design for each subject, in that in one REM period of the night the subject was woken after no electrical stimulation and asked to report. If subjects were merely trying to please the experimenter, then accounts of becoming lucid would also be given at these wakenings.

The results of the study were very good. Even though only one night per subject was permitted, half of the participants reported becoming lucid from the point the shocks were perceived to waking—a minute or so later.

Successful induction

Case 1: (6.40 a.m.)

This subject was having an ordinary dream where she was working in a large department store:

I reached the top of the store and there was a line of young children filing somewhere to my right out of my vision. I'd just managed to persuade one lad who was unwilling to move to follow the others when I felt the impulses. I found myself, still in the dream, then unaccountably riding down an escalator—still apparently in the department store—holding on to a thin model duck with a yellow ribbon round its neck!

I knew I was lucid and dreaming and was horrified to note that this was the best I could do. I tried hard to make the dream more my idea of heaven, but only succeeded in making the yellow string longer.

Actually, this was not bad for a first try. The main objective, to establish the awareness of dreaming, had worked well. Skill at controlling dreams comes through trial and error practice (Chapter 9).

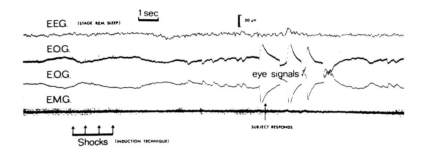

Fig. 13.
Lucid-dream induction in the sleep-lab. Electrical pulses to the wrist are incorporated into the dream without causing waking and are recognized as the lucidity 'cue'. The subject, now perfectly aware of being in a dream, responds by making eye-movement signals

Incidentally, a few minutes before this subject's dream, I had passed a lift-shaft in another part of the building and noticed that a bird was trapped inside. I thought this was a strange event and wondered whether it might be telepathically conveyed to the sleeping subject. (At that time I was also concerned with dream-telepathy experiments.) It struck me as odd then, when the induced lucid dream report referred to travelling on a moving staircase with a duck! I had made no mention to the subject of the bird trapped in the lift, and she could not have heard any noise from the creature. Another point of similarity is that the dream setting was a department store, and the sleep-lab was in the psychology department (mere coincidence, or something more?).

In fact this subject was Susan Mott, a journalist at that time for the *Hull Daily Mail*. She wrote a large piece about her experiences in the sleep-lab for that newspaper,[1] and another item was published in the national *Daily Mail*.[2]

Case 2

Lucidity was induced several times in this subject.

(a) 6 a.m.

The subject reported that she was dreaming of being in a newsagent's shop when she felt the pulses and signalled. The imagery on this occasion, though, was not very vivid. Some 'alpha' brain activity entered the EEG record at that time, indicating waking, but REM was then re-entered until she was roused.

(b) 7.45 a.m.

Clear signals appeared in the polygraphic chart after stimulation. The subject was on a railway station, coming home from holiday. On receiving the pulses, she found herself on the train. She knew she was dreaming then, and signalled. The quality of the imagery was reported to be good.

(c) 8.15 a.m.

The subject was dreaming of plugging in an electric kettle when she felt the pulses and became lucid. The imagery was excellent and 'lasted several seconds'.

(d) 9.15 a.m.

Here, the subject was playing with matches. One was struck when the first pulse was received. The imagery was vivid.

Case 3: (1.30 a.m.)

Three sets of pulses were received within the dream by this subject, who responded each time by making ocular signals. On waking, she stated that she became aware of dreaming when the pulses arrived while she was watching a person being 'wired up' for a sleep experiment. The person appeared to be in a transparent cage. The thought came to the subject, 'Beam me up Scotty' (that is, from ordinary dreaming to lucidity).

Case 4: (5.45 a.m.)

This subject was dreaming about her boy-friend. They were together on a beach, and she noticed the clear blue sky. Actually, she did not feel any pulses but realized she was dreaming and signalled, which was shortly after the pulses were administered. It occurred to her to try to alter the dream in some way and she was thinking about how to achieve this when she was woken up.

Case 5

3.30 a.m.

The shocks were felt, but no visual content was reported.

7.15 a.m.

The subject was dreaming of talking to me and someone else. She felt some pulses and became lucid, briefly. Then she was running along a street and felt the pulses. She 'took a chance' and signalled back while continuing to run. She had insight into dreaming then and was very interested in observing what was happening, with full consciousness. The imagery was very bright and clear. At another point in this extended period of dreaming, she was in a canteen talking to me when the pulses were perceived. She responded by signalling. A children's book was seen very clearly. All the words in Chapter 1 began with 'a', and so on, throughout the book.

Case 6

Lucidity was established in two REM periods with this subject, but a false awakening happened during the first occasion.

(a) 3.30 a.m.

I felt the shocks and gave the eye signals. I thought you came in and pulled the duvet back and asked what I had been dreaming about. I then felt another set of shocks and kept on giving eye signals. While giving these, I thought it strange that you had come in and did not notice the eye movements on the record. The dream was very dark and the imagery virtually nonexistent. I started to look around but could not see very much. I then woke up.

(b) 6 a.m.

I was in the sleep-lab and the experimenter was an old boy-friend called Tony. There was a girl dressed in a bra and pants and saying, 'Why I came from Florida to this place I will never know!' That is when I felt the shocks. I signalled and went on with the dream because it wasn't an unpleasant situation. I was getting dressed in the bedroom and I heard Tony's ex-wife ask him if we were having an affair. A girl, very blonde and looking like Dolly Parton, looked in from a sun-roof in the ceiling and asked us if we would like coffee. The colour in the dream was very good and the imagery clear. I was conscious of being in a dream after the pulses.

Lucidity followed by rapid waking

There were two occasions when this happened.

Case 1: (4.30 a.m.)

I was dreaming of being in a park behind my parents' home. My father was with me. The imagery was very vivid. I was bending down to put my hand into a stream, and felt the shocks. I realized instantly that I was dreaming and was surprised that my father was in fact a dream image. The imagery went and I started to signal, but woke.

Case 2: (6.30 a.m.)

I was dreaming of being in a student house at Hull. The imagery was fairly bright. A friend from home was there. I turned round to talk to her, when I felt the pulses. I began to signal, but woke up.

Non-realization

Here, the subject perceived one of the pulses but it was not enough to trigger lucidity:

> I felt one slight throb in my arm and I didn't signal because I didn't think it could have been the shock. I debated with myself feeling sure I was awake, but then doubt crept in and I wondered if I could possibly be dreaming. I could see people walking about, and I was walking too, so I decided to look around for evidence. I suddenly saw a brief glimpse of a vivid picture—like one slide taken from a colour film. I was looking into a small paved square. To my left was a large building and to my right a more modern office block. A stream of people were crossing the square and I particularly noticed one girl with long blonde hair. I felt it could be a university campus. Colour was vague, but the left was dark brick-red and the figures were mostly wearing blue and white. The picture was 'frozen', and I woke up when I heard you enter the sleep-lab bedroom.

Dreaming the pulses

One subject dreamed that she had received the pulses and became lucid anyway! In fact, earlier in the night she had a false awakening. She 'woke' and tried to call out to me, but found she could not do so. That made her realize she was dreaming. She signalled anyway. Unfortunately, the polygraph was not running at that time.

This subject then dreamed that I, and another person, came into the sleep-lab bedroom and sexually assaulted her. She stated, 'I was not enjoying it, but I thought, "As it's a lucid dream, I might as well enjoy it." ' She then woke up and called out to me (3.15 a.m.).

At 6.20 a.m., this subject called out to me that she had 'felt the pulses, and signalled'. This was strange because no pulses whatsoever had been administered, and the chart was not running. This point is noteworthy because it illustrates how strong the element of expectation or suggestion can be in such circumstances. It was on the basis of this and other observations that I developed the 'F.A.S.T.' technique for experimental induction. This is a method (which needs an assistant) that might occasionally work with some people (Chapter 8).

In one person, the sensory thresholds seemed too low, so that waking always followed stimulation.

Three subjects had to be discarded from the experiment due to equipment failure. No cases of subjects reporting recent lucidity were found in the catch-trials. Two subjects were not given a catch-trial, because I fell asleep!

Misperception

Another effect of expectation that I have noticed is that sometimes subjects will erroneously perceive an external source of stimulation (not the pulses) as the electrical shocks, presumably because they are expected. It is a type of misperception:

> I had a dream that the dream machine pulses went off as I was meeting a composer. Then I was immediately woken by the alarm clock. I had thought, 'These are the dream-machine pulses to make me lucid.'

Misapprehension

A common misunderstanding about the dream machine is that before sleep you somehow 'programme in' the dream you wish to have. Even with the lucid function that is not the case—but I might work on it!

An independent confirmation!

When the dream machine had received its first publicity, one US electronic expert decided to construct a version of the device which he reported was workable. He reported that the number of his lucid dreams had increased very considerably as a consequence of using the unit, and he was now a frequent lucid dreamer. He, naturally, was very pleased with my invention!

Television test

In 1981, an early model of the dream machine was tested by a team from the British television programme *Newsnight*. They provided three people with the unit, but only for a very few nights each. One of the subjects, David James from Oxford, was able to report that he had become lucid several times with the unit, and looked pleased as he stated this on the air! This was quite a reasonable rate of success in view of the shortness of the test period, the lack of adequate instructions, and absence of any prior training with the device. The producer of the programme also tried it for one night, and rang to congratulate me the next day that the machine had made him become lucid in a dream. The presenter stated that he had not become lucid during his brief trial period, but he was sure that there was 'something in it'.

Versions

Two separate versions of the dream machine have been developed out of much experimentation. A small, simple model monitors respiratory rate to identify dreaming sleep and automatically activates an incrementing audible waking alarm. The unit includes set long- and short-timers, so that it becomes operational after several hours and permits a few minutes of dreaming. The breathing rate at which the device triggers is also fixed. There is a 'test' mode in which the device tests all its electronic functions and gives a bleep if everything is working correctly.

An automatic nightmare detector functions continuously, even when the long-timer is running, so that if a much increased breathing rate is registered, indicating a possible nightmare, the waking alarm will sound to protect the user.

The dream machine proper has several variable features so that it may be more closely adjusted to the user's physiological characteristics. Both long- and short-timers are completely variable, and the triggering respiratory rate may be 'dialled in' by thumbwheel switches. The strength of the electrical pulses (meant to cue lucidity) is alterable over a wide range. An override facility is part of the design, so that by pressing the 'stop alarm' button on the top of the unit the long-timer is cut out and the machine begins to function in its set mode immediately.

The mode of operation may be switched to:

(a) TEST—where individual electronic functions may be tested;
(b) NIGHTMARE—where the device will waken the user

immediately a predetermined breathing rate is attained; and
(c) DREAM—where the short-timer, governing the amount of
further dreaming allowed, becomes operational.

In mode (c), the device is also switchable to LUCID, so that the
pulses are administered and a set period of dreaming elapses
between stimulation and the waking alarm.

In a sense, the dream machine and user have to get to know
each other. It is a process of tuning. Individuals are physiologically unique, but the device is flexible in its different functions,
so that by trial and error the best settings for a particular section
of the sleep period can be established.

Generally, the later dream periods are 'best' to be woken from,
and for experimental lucidity induction, but not with everyone.
Some people prefer to have a high setting on the short-timer,
others the exact opposite. The triggering breathing rate may be
lower for dream periods later in the sleep period than in the early
ones, so this should be accounted for in such home experiments.

It is important to get into the habit of always noting down any
dreams that were in progress when the waking alarm sounds.
This increases dream recall and helps to produce a psychological
'set' reinforcing interest in the experiments with the unit.
Contact with others interested in dreams is also beneficial and
motivating.

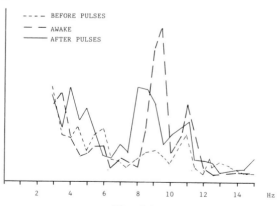

Fig. 14.
Brain-wave power at different frequencies before and after
pulses, and awake. The graph shows that in this subject there
was some slow 'alpha' activity when the pulses were received
but that it is not like that of wakefulness

Because people are so very different, both physiologically and psychologically, the degree of success of the lucidity aspect is not readily predictable. A period of training, to establish the optimum dream-waking parameters, is sensible before moving on to experimental lucidity induction. Motivation and interest are also significant elements in the equation.

Dream power

There are certain groups in society who would be especially benefited by developing the ability to dream lucidly. I am thinking of those persons who are in some way confined or disabled and so cannot experience the rich variety of events that constitute living for most of us. A door would be opened for these people to the conscious experience of the limitless wonders in the dream world.

The physically disabled are often frustrated as to what they can achieve in life. Their motility may be severely limited and social interactions greatly curtailed. It would surely be therapeutic for such patients to harness lucid dreaming, so as to gain release from their bodily restraints. Why should they not walk, run, fly, make love and do anything else in their dream body?

There is also a case for prisoners to learn to become lucid in dreams. While long prison sentences no doubt rid society of many people who have behaved wrongly, they also impose a cruelty, that of unnatural confinement, on these offenders. Perhaps long-term prisoners should be encouraged to take up lucid dreaming as an acceptable and humane form of recreation.

For the rest of us, why not learn the art of dreaming in its most advanced form, and enrich our lives further by its marvels?

References
1. *Hull Daily Mail*, 28 May 1980, p. 5.
2. *Daily Mail*, 29 August 1980, p. 12.

6

The Dream Machine and the Paranormal

There is no question that throughout recorded history dreams have been associated with paranormal phenomena, in particular, telepathy, clairvoyance and premonitions. In ancient civilizations, it was believed that messages could be conveyed via dreams. In ancient Egypt, 'dream incubation' was practised whereby a person requiring future information from a deity would, after various rituals, sleep in a temple or 'Serapeum', and experience a meaningful dream. Its interpretation by skilled priests, would provide knowledge of events yet to happen.

Cases of what we would now term dream telepathy or premonitions were recorded by the Greeks and Romans.[1] Cicero, for instance, described how a man called Simonides found a body on a beach and paid for it to be buried. At the time Simonides was planning to go on a sea voyage, but he experienced a warning dream in which the buried man urged him not to travel because the ship would sink. Simonides took heed of the dream and later discovered that the ship was indeed lost and everyone aboard drowned.

The Old Testament of the Bible contains some 15 prophetic dreams. The most famous one was that of the Pharaoh who dreamed of the seven fat and thin cattle, interpreted by Joseph to represent seven years of abundance followed by seven years of famine (Genesis 41–43).

The interesting seventeenth-century *Miscellanies* written by John Aubrey, F.R.S. contains accounts of strange happenings that he collected,[2] including apparently paranormal dreams. One little known fact he relates tells of how the astronomer Edmund Halley (of comet fame), before he went to St Helena for some observations, dreamed of seeing the island. Later, he was amazed to find the place exactly as he had foreseen.

There are countless recorded cases that have occurred since. One was the dream of a Cornish mines superintendent, John Williams, in May 1812, in which he was in the House of Commons.[3] A small man dressed in a blue coat and white waistcoat entered. Another person, dressed in a 'snuff-coloured' coat with metal buttons, took a pistol from under his coat and shot the small man. On enquiring who the victim was, Williams was told that it was Mr Spencer Perceval, the Prime Minister. Williams had the same dream three times that night. He was so alarmed that he felt inclined to travel to London and warn the Prime Minister, but friends dissuaded him. A little over a week later, John Bellingham assassinated Spencer Perceval in the House of Commons. Apparently the items of clothing tallied excatly with those seen in the dream.

Another notable premonitory dream,[4] which was well attested, concerned that momentous event in history, the assassination of the Archduke Ferdinand and his wife Sophie in Sarajevo. Bishop Joseph de Lanyi had a dream at 3.30 a.m. on the morning of 28 June 1914 in which he received a letter from the archduke. The letterhead illustrated a scene of the assassination, involving a motor vehicle. The letter stated that he and his wife would be killed the next day.

The bishop communicated the dream to several people, and even held a special mass for the couple. The murders did actually happen later that day. The event contributed to the start of the First World War.

Hearne's survey

The field of premonitions is one that I have studied extensively.[5] Some 40 per cent of psychic phenomena are precognitive, and 60 per cent or so of these come in the form of dreams. As a result of an appeal in a British national newspaper, I received many hundreds of cases of premonitions and a sample of the respondents were given questionnaires and personality tests to complete. I also thoroughly investigated certain specific cases and percipients. Some 90 per cent of persons reporting premonitions are female, although there is probably a reporting bias in that figure, in that men may be more reluctant to admit having foreknowledge. Most reported cases concern death or injury:

I went with my sister to Germany for a two-week stay with my niece and her husband who lived in married quarters. There was to be a party, but the night before I had a dream. All the furniture had been arranged along the walls. A couple came in and asked if we had heard of the accident at the camp that morning. Three soldiers had been killed. The dream was so vivid that I asked if such news had been mentioned the previous night, but it had not. That night, we arrived at the party. The room was exactly as I had seen it. We sat down for a drink and the same couple came in. I knew straight away what would happen. They said the very words that I had heard in my dream. My niece, her husband and my sister looked at me open-mouthed. 'You mentioned that this morning!' they said. (M. Ellis)

Such accounts are rampant in the population, yet official science ignores the evidence—a curiously unscientific stance that will surely seem incomprehensible to subsequent generations.

Most subjects reported that premonitory dreams had a certain quality, often of great vividness, that distinguished them from ordinary dreams.

One woman, Barbara Garwell, whose cases were investigated in detail, dreamed of the assassination of President Sadat, the attempt on the life of President Reagan, and of a fire on the SS *Achille Lauro*—all with a latency period of three weeks between dream and event.

To overcome the objection that perhaps only these premonitions that come to fruition are reported by percipients ('preferential selection'), I got Barbara Garwell to send me any premonitions she 'received', immediately, throughout one year (1982). In all, 52 premonitions were received. Later, two judges looked through newspapers covering one month after each premonition and looked for any items that corresponded with that premonition, awarding it a mark (0–8) for accuracy.[6]

The judges did the same with the premonitions for a different control year (1981 or 1983). They were led to believe that half the accounts were from the actual year and the others from a control, randomly mixed. This was so that they would not develop a conviction that one particular year was the correct one. A statistical test was applied in an extremely cautious form. It revealed that, even so, the ratings for the actual year were higher than for the control year at a level which approached statistical significance. This was a promising result for the first test of its kind ever conducted.

In fact, though, perhaps the best evidence came from further demonstrations in those premonitions that appeared to achieve fruition of the consistent latency period of three weeks with her dreams and three days associated with waking imagery premonitions. Just to illustrate this last mentioned category, Barbara always sent her premonition reports by post, but in May 1982 she telephoned me urgently (she had not done so before) and told me of an imagery-premonition of someone, who she thought was the Pope, being attacked. Three days later, at the Fatima shrine in Portugal, a man attempted to stab the Pope with a bayonet; it was reported in the news.

Anecdotal cases of premonition, mostly having arisen in dreams, are commonplace in society. They are generally reported by people who have experienced many other cases. Spot-checks on percipients, by checking with witnesses, have in my experience always confirmed the reports.

Dream telepathy in the sleep-lab

A series of fascinating dream-telepathy experiments was undertaken at the Maimonides Hospital in New York in the 1960s.[7] The principal researchers, Montague Ullman and Stanley Krippner, produced existing evidence of telepathic effects manifesting in the dream state. Typically, the 'receiver' person was wired up in the sleep-laboratory and was woken for dream reports after each REM period. A 'transmitter' person attempted to influence the dreams of the subject by concentrating on certain material that had been selected by a random process. This happened, with different target material, over several nights. Later, the subject and 'naive' judges rated the amount of similarity between each night's dream reports and each of a set of possible target material, among which was the correct one. Statistical tests then determined the likelihood of telepathy having been involved.

Thus, in one study over seven nights, using the best subject from a previous 'screening' experiment, the target picture-prints used by the 'transmitter' were:

1	*Bedtime* by Keane	Miss
2	*Yellow Rabbi* by Chagall	Hit
3	*The Sacrament of the Last Supper* by Dali	Hit
4	*School of the Dance* by Degas	Hit
5	*Paris Through a Window* by Chagall	Hit

6	*Persistence of Memory* by Dali	Hit
7	*Apples and Oranges* by Cézanne	Miss

A second study with this same person also produced a statistically significant result.

Foreknowledge was studied in two experiments using the English sensitive Malcolm Bessent. In these, the subject's dreams were recorded for a night. Then, the next day, a randomly selected 'happening' was planned and enacted. One of the targets was the painting *Hospital Corridor at St Remy* by Van Gogh. The multi-sensory event the next day included Bessent watching slides of paintings by mental patients, taking a pill in water, smelling disinfectant, and being led through a corridor. The first study covered eight nights, and the second totalled 16 nights. Both gave statistically significant results in favour of the paranormal hypothesis. It should just be mentioned that, theoretically at least, instead of precognition happening it might have been that Bessent was affecting the later target selection using powers of PK (psychokinesis). Either way the results are thought provoking.

Given these considerable indications that the dream state harbours some remarkable psi phenomena, and since the dream machine makes dreams so much more accessible, there is obviously a great potential for psi experimentation using the device. Moreover, such studies are well within the capability of the enthusiastic amateur experimenting at home.

The first lucidity and psi test in the sleep-lab

Revelling in the never before explored field of communication from the lucid dream state, one little study that I conducted in my Ph.D. work investigated dream telepathy. Whereas in ordinary dreams the 'transmitter' person tries to alter the dream content in the 'receiver', with lucid dreams the dreamer, knowing full well that he/she is dreaming, can concentrate on making guesses as to the target material and signal out those guesses. If there was something greatly enhancing about telepathy in REM sleep, then it would be revealed by a simple experiment.

Before sleep, the lucid dream subject (A.W.) was told of my intention to try to 'send' a four-digit random number when he became lucid and had signalled that fact by eye movements that were registered in the polygraphic record. He was told he should then look around the dream environment for any numbers, or simply guess some and signal those out by making corresponding numbers of extreme eye movements. In order to reduce the amount of signalling, which might have interfered with the dream, the numbers would be low (1 to 5).

When the subject was asleep, I selected a four-digit random number using random number tables. At 6.30 a.m., the standard 'lucidity' signals came through in the chart and I began to concentrate on the number. On waking, the subject reported a dream in which he had seen pebbles and wood-grain with extraordinary clarity. He had seen a three-digit number stamped on something. It was perhaps 156, but he woke while signalling the last digit. The chart record revealed that the digits 1 and 5 (or 6) were communicated. In fact, the target was 2444, so there was no success there.

On the second occasion of this telepathy test, the subject found himself in a dream where there were numbers on gates. He saw one number which might have been 223, but he was confused by seeing many numbers. The number 253 was in the record, while the target was 3352. At least, the same digits were in both numbers. Unfortunately, pressure of other work meant that this study could not be continued, but it is quite certain that this general technique will be a useful method of investigating dream-psi in the future. On reflection, it would probably have been better to try to transmit pictures, as in the Maimonides work, and then see how they corresponded with dream settings.

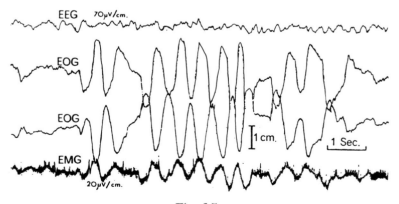

Fig. 15.
Signals from within a lucid dream in a telepathy experiment

A precognition revealed by the dream machine?[8]

Pamela Green was trying out a dream machine, using it in the 'nightmare' mode, so that she was woken immediately her breathing rate hit a pre-set value. It was at a low level, so that, effectively, emotional peaks in ordinary dreams were being detected.

On being woken by the device at those points, Pamela noted down what she had been dreaming. On the fifth night, she was roused while experiencing a vivid, coloured dream. She made brief notes, and told me about the dream in detail the next day. Pamela stated:

> I was in a high building. There was a large plate-glass window, and a balustrade with a wooden top. There were pink and grey zig-zag curtains. I looked out of the window, down a hill. There were buildings and roads, with traffic. At the bottom of the hill I saw a building which I 'knew' was a cinema. It had lights on it, but I could not make out the name. The building I was in had two entrances (on the left and right corners) and I 'knew' that parking was not possible in the front and that I had come from a car-park at the side and had to walk the whole length of the front to an entrance that was open.

Two days after the dream, Pamela visited Bradford in West Yorkshire. She had been there years before, when she was 12, and had appeared nightly in a pantomime for a week. On arrival this time, Pamela and her travelling friend decided to go to the National Museum of Photography. Parking was not possible in front of the building and a walk was necessary from the side to the far front corner entrance of the building. The other entrance was locked.

The couple went up to the fifth floor of the modern structure, and Pamela was utterly amazed at seeing the details of her dream—although the curtains were not there. From the window she could see the scene just as in her dream, and where the cinema was in the dream was a real cinema with lights spelling out the word 'Odeon'.

Pamela had a strong sense of recognition, and she telephoned me excitedly about the strange episode on her return.

Now strictly speaking, a definite explanation in terms of pre-cognition is not permissible because, for instance, it just may have been that Pamela had seen some photos of the building and the area in some display she had not remembered consciously. Nevertheless, it is certainly conceivable at least that the dream contained precognitive material. The dream machine of course 'selected' the dream which otherwise would have continued and Pamela would almost certainly not have recalled anything about it the next day. So, here was some evidence that the dream machine might prove to be a useful tool for parapsychologists in selecting precognitive material in dreams. Pamela was woken at a moment of physiological arousal, with an elevated breathing rate—but not that of a nightmare. It is possible that this state of moderate physiological activation may reflect the typical bodily condition associated with psi dreams. If that is so, their identification might be facilitated using the device.

A home dream telepathy study using the dream machine

The dream machine was employed in a dream telepathy study in which the 'receiver' person was Nerys Dee, the well-known dream interpreter who has written a book on dreams.[9] It was a long-distance experiment in that Nerys lives some 150 miles from me. The experimental set-up was straightforward. Nerys used the dream machine on eight non-consecutive nights. The long-timer on the device was set so that the machine did not become operational until after 5 a.m. It was switched to the 'nightmare' mode, so that Nerys would be woken at emotional peaks in dreams (Pam's experience indicated that those moments might be conducive to psi). On being woken by the device, Nerys would note down any dream that was going on at that point.

Nerys and I conferred to arrange mutually convenient nights. On these experimental nights, I concentrated on the target material between 5 and 7 a.m. An assistant prepared the targets. These consisted of eight pictures per experimental night, one of which was selected using an elaborate randomizing process involving random-number tables. The target pictures were taken from magazines, and were meant to be as distinct as possible from each other. Each of the targets was duplicated. The ones to be used by me were correspondingly numbered for selection by

Fig. 16.
**Dream interpreter Nerys Dee linked up to the dream machine
in a dream-telepathy study conducted by the author**

the randomizing process. Each batch of duplicates was placed in
a single envelope to be sent to Nerys after the night's experiment.

Just before the experiment began each morning at 5 a.m., I
selected a target envelope by the following procedure. A die was
thrown to select one of six blocks of random numbers (from
pages 12 and 13 of *Cambridge Elementary Statistical Tables* by
C.V. Lindley and J.C.P. Miller, C.U.P., 1971). It was thrown again
to select a sub-group of 40 digits. The rows were inspected until
a digit 1–8 was encountered. The envelope bearing that number
was chosen as the target picture.

Now the reason why Nerys was sent duplicates of the targets
was that if she received the night's batch including the selected
target, she might have unconsciously determined that one

because, say, it might have had more wear and tear than the others.

Nerys herself then studied the batch of eight pictures—one of which was the actual target—in the last experimental night, and compared each one with her dream report. She ranked each picture in order of correspondence with her dream, and gave a confidence measure too. Those rankings between 1 and 4 would be deemed to be 'hits', while those between 5 and 8 were 'misses'.

As a precaution against fraud on my part, at the end of the whole experiment both Nerys and I sent copies of our respective data to the Secretary of the Society for Psychical Research.

Night	Rank of actual target	Rank of actual target	Hit (1–4) Miss (5–8)
1	7	10%	M
2	6	20%	M
3	4	30%	H
4	3	30%	H
5	6	9%	M
6	4	35%	H
7	6	20%	M
8	6	25%	M

List of Ranks and Ratings by Nerys

Nerys reported that the dream machine functioned flawlessly and that was woken during vivid dreaming on each of the experimental nights. However, the results of the study were not statistically significant. None of the pictures scored a direct 'hit' (i.e. ranked 1), and the ratings of coincidence were generally low. So this particular study did not provide evidence in support of dream telepathy under the circumstances prevailing.

Not that that matters. The main value of this study was to demonstrate that the device can be used in a simple yet valid dream-telepathy experiment by anyone at home. Other users, perhaps with exceptional psychic abilities, might produce some really worth-while results. At least, the technique is now available.

The dream machine and the telephone

Suppose you owned a dream machine and wished to perform a

simple dream-telepathy experiment with someone who was at a distance. How could that person know *when* you were dreaming, so that they could 'transmit' or 'receive' information? One way, as in the previous experiment, is for the awake person to send or receive over a long period, when dreaming is likely, but it is tedious for that individual.

A method has been developed, however, that overcomes the problem. What happens is that when the dream machine 'triggers' on detecting dreaming, it can switch on an electronic automatic telephone-dialling device. Thus the other participant in the experiment may be contacted—literally anywhere in the world. A telephone call would be received, giving a recorded message, or an electronic tone would be transmitted that would be recognized as a signal. He or she may then concentrate, either to influence the dreamer's dream in a certain direction, or to try to detect the nature of the dream. After a variable amount of dreaming time, the device will then awaken the user, and the details may be noted. The technique has been fully tested and shown to work perfectly satisfactorily.[10]

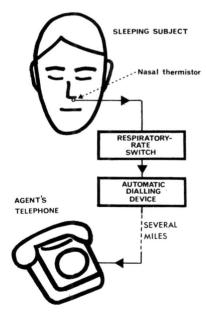

Fig. 17.
Schematic diagram of experimental set-up

Beyond that arrangement, another possibility exists. A dreamer who becomes lucid, either spontaneously or by using the device's pulses method, could make some rapid breaths (respiration under voluntary control in REM sleep) and so trigger the telephone-dialling apparatus. The great advantage here is that the dreamer—paralysed, yet conscious in a dream environment —is fully aware of taking part in a telepathy experiment. An effort could then be made, say, to 'fly' to the other participant and see the target material.

An even more mind-boggling idea is that on becoming lucid one person, using the telephone link connected to another person's dream machine, could trigger the pulses in that second device. If the other individual was in dreaming sleep at that time, lucidity might ensue there too. Who knows what might happen between two people, both lucid at the same time and knowing that to be the case?

A problem about obtaining possible telepathic or precognitive information in lucid dreams is how to manoeuvre the dream to that purpose. There are several possible ways. A dream character may be questioned, say, as to the date and any news about the world or a particular person (it must be stated, though, that dream characters are not always that helpful!). If a newsagent's shop is nearby, one can look at newspaper headlines and the date—it may be in the future.

One method that a friend, Sheelah Furman, uses with great success is to use a telephone in the lucid-dream scenery. She gave an example of how, realizing she was dreaming, she decided to telephone a friend who was in India. They 'conversed' for some time, during which her friend said he had been very ill with a fever and gave details of the disease. On his return to England he confirmed that he was indeed ill with those same symptoms at that time. While the dream state may be conducive to psi, for the best results the dream may well have to be 'tuned' in such a way for the information to emerge.

It should not be forgotten that dreams can also, apparently, foretell favourable events!

In the early hours of the morning, I had a dream of someone telling me a horse was going to win, and its name was Bean (something). Over breakfast, I asked my husband if he had heard of a horse by that name. He said he hadn't, and we joked about it because I have never had a dream about a horse winning and I am hopeless at picking a

winner at anything. My husband sent my son to get the daily paper.
My husband said he couldn't see a horse of that name listed.
As I sat down for a coffee at 10.30 a.m., I grabbed the paper and I
straight away saw the horse listed—Bean Boy. I was so excited, I rang
my mother, my sister, my brother-in-law, and a friend, Harry, who
likes a little flutter. They each placed a £1 bet on the horse. We put
£20 of the mortgage money on it. The horse won at 7 to 1. I was
thrilled.

Marion Threadgold

It's impossible to say whether a single premonition was genuine
or not, because one on its own could just have been that one-in-
a-billion chance coincidence, but the fact that some individuals
come up repeatedly with witnessed cases indicates that precognition is a fact of life—and should be a fact of science.

From a practical viewpoint, a lucid dreamer wishing to find,
say, the winner of a horse-race yet to take place (as an experiment) should guide the dream to a situation where such information could logically (in the dream) be revealed. One suggested
way of accomplishing this would be to construct a 'time machine'
in the dream scenery which could be 'programmed' to show you
the future horse-race or give a running commentary. The device
would probably have to be refined over several different lucid
dreams, by trial and error. Touching on science fiction (or is it?),
perhaps dreams can also facilitate psychokinesis, or mind-over-
matter powers. Is it possible to visit a place in a lucid dream and
cause some change which is then observed to happen in the
waking world? We have no idea what might be feasible in
dreams. There is considerable evidence that paranormal phenomena exist, and it may be that precognition, telepathy and PK
might be greatly enhanced in such a state.

I understand that the US military is somewhat interested in
lucid dreaming, for 'remote-viewing', dream-entering of individuals, and remote PK. The CIA's former head, William Casey,
was fascinated by the topic of parapsychology.

At the annual Conference of the Parapsychology Foundation at
New Orleans in 1984, I read a paper entitled 'Lucid dreams and
psi research',[11] which pointed out the advantages of the dream
machine in parapsychological studies. Parapsychologists are
certainly aware of the potential, but there is also great scope for
ordinary lay persons who possess a device to conduct their own
researches. Among them could be some very gifted subjects!

References

1. Dodds, E.R. (1971) Supernormal phenomena in classical antiquity. *Proceedings of the Society for Psychical Research*, 55 (205), 189–237.
2. Aubrey, J. (1890; orig. 1696) *Miscellanies*. Library of Old Authors, Reeves & Turner, London.
3. Sidgwick, H. (1988) On the evidence for premonitions. *Proceedings of the Society for Psychical Research*, 5, 288–354.
4. Pauli, H. (1966) *The Secret of Sarajevo*. Collins, London.
5. Hearne, K.M.T. (1989) *Visions of the Future*. Aquarian Press, Wellingborough, Northants.
6. Hearne, K.M.T. (1986) An analysis of premonitions deposited over one year, from an apparently gifted subject. *Journal of the Society for Psychical Research*, 53 (804), 376–82.
7. Ullman, M., Krippner, S., & Vaughan, A. (1973) *Dream Telepathy*. MacMillan, New York.
8. Hearne, K.M.T. (1985) An ostensible precognition using a 'dream machine'. *Journal of the Society for Psychical Research*, 53 (799), 338–40.
9. Dee, N. (1984) *Your Dreams and What They Mean*. Aquarian Press, Wellingborough, Northants.
10. Hearne, K.M.T. (1982) An automated technique for studying psi in home 'lucid' dreams. *Journal of the Society for Psychical Research*, 51 (791), 303–304.
11. Hearne, K.M.T. (1984) Lucid dreams and psi research. In *Current Trends in Psi Research*. Proceedings of an International Conference held in New Orleans, Louisiana, August 13–14, eds. B. Shapin & L. Coly. Parapsychology Foundation, Inc., New York, pp192–218.

7

Dream Potentials

The dream state has a reputation for being the source of many scientific and artistic ideas. One of the most exciting prospects about dreaming is that perhaps we could learn to exploit that great treasure-house of originality—particularly using lucid dreams. Then, who knows what novel concepts and works of art might successfully be transferred from that inner universe to this world?

In science, one of the great examples of inspiration in dreams was provided by the chemist Friedrich Kekulé, who comprehended the structure of the benzene molecule as a result of a hypnagogic dream. He wrote:

> I turned my chair to the fire and dozed. Again the atoms were gambolling before my eyes. This time the smaller groups kept modestly in the background. My mental eye, rendered more acute by visions of this kind, could now distinguish larger structures, of manifold confirmations; long rows, sometimes more closely fitted together, all twining and twisting in snakelike motion. But look! What was that? One of the snakes had seized hold of its own tail, and the form whirled mockingly before my eyes. As if by a flash of lightning, I awoke.

Kekulé had realized that the benzene molecule had a ringlike shape. It was a milestone discovery in organic chemistry. Kekulé later told an assembled conference, 'Gentlemen, we must learn to dream!'

The first person to show that chemicals are transported at the junctions of nerves to pass on the stimulus was Otto Loewi, who won the Nobel prize for his discovery. He had a hunch in 1903 that such a process operated, but he could not think of a way to test the idea. Several years later, in a dream, he hit upon a method based on a technique he had used more recently on something else. Unfortunately, although he had made some notes on waking, Loewi could not read them, and could not adequately recall the dream. The next night, however, the dream was repeated. Lowei conducted the experiment. Essentially, he was able to show, using two frog hearts, one with nerves intact, the other without, that after stimulation of the former (increasing or decreasing the beat), transferring the salt solution from the first to the second heart correspondingly affected the beat of the second. Clearly, this was due to chemical rather than electrical means.

The archaeologist Herman Hilprecht managed to solve problems in the dream state. One case was when he was working on the decipherment of two fragments of agate, which seemed to come from two finger rings and which had cuneiform markings. Hilprecht had a dream in which a tall priest guided him to the treasure chamber of a temple and informed him how the two pieces belonged together and were not finger rings but earrings, made from an agate cylinder. It was later confirmed that the two pieces did fit together as stated in the dream.

Elias Howe invented the lock-stitch sewing machine. He had been faced with a great problem in the design concerning its needle, which had a hole in the middle of its shank. It is said that Howe had a nightmare in which he was captured by savages and ordered to complete the machine immediately. He noticed that the spears of the guards had eye-shaped holes at the point. Immediately he realized that that was the correct position for the hole in machine needles. Howe awoke, leapt out of bed, and constructed the first successful model.

Many of the great composers—Mozart, Schumann and Saint-Saëns, for instance—heard original themes in their dreams and included them in their compositions. Some interesting illustrations have been reported. Beethoven fell asleep in a coach one day and dreamed of travelling through several countries, arriving at Jerusalem. A repetitive piece of music then came into his mind associated with the words 'O Tobias, O Tobias, Dominus Haslinger O! O! O Tobias!' He could not recall the music on waking, but the next day the experience was repeated and that time he remembered, so he wrote it down.

The Italian violinist/composer Giuseppe Tartini described to the astronomer Joseph Lalande a dream he had in which the devil had become Tartini's slave. He handed Satan a violin, thinking that he could not play the instrument, but was amazed when the devil played a sonata 'of such exquisite beauty as surpassed the boldest flights of my imagination'. Unfortunately, most of the music was forgotten on waking, except for a trill which Tartini included in his work *The Devil's Sonata*.

The French philosopher Descartes had three significant dreams on one night in 1619, which he interpreted and thereby came to an understanding of his aims in philosophy. In the third dream, for instance, he observed a poetry book and a dictionary on a table. One verse he noticed stated, 'What way of life should I follow?' Someone appeared and asked him to look up a poem which began, 'Yes, No', but he could not find the piece. Those books and the man disappeared, and Descartes apparently became dream-lucid. While still asleep, he tried to seek a meaning to the dream, and thought it represented the fusion of philosophy and wisdom, and that poets may reveal more wisdom than philosophers.

On waking, he further considered that the 'Yes, No' referred to Truth and Falsity in Pythagoras, and so saw it as 'truth and falsity in knowledge and the profane sciences'. He summarized the dream as 'the Spirit of Truth who had sought to open to him the treasures of all the sciences by this dream'.

In the field of literature, dreams have provided excellent ideas which have formed the bases of stories and plays. Robert Louis Stevenson, who wrote many vivid tales of adventure, such as *Treasure Island* and *Kidnapped*, found early on in life that he could dream whole stories, recall them well and write them down. For his classic book *The Strange Case of Dr Jekyll and Mr Hyde*, Stevenson made considerable use of a plot that came upon him in a dream. In the dream, Hyde, who was being chased after committing a crime, took a potion and changed to the other character. From a few scenes, and the basic idea of a potion to alter a person's character and appearance, his book was formed. It was a superb example of the exploitation of dreams.

The poetic masterpiece *Kubla Khan* was composed by Samuel Taylor Coleridge during vivid dreaming, and written down on waking. Coleridge had fallen asleep while reading the following from *Purchas his Pilgrimage*: 'In Xamdu did Cublai Can build a stately Palace, encompassing sixteene miles of plaine ground with a wall, wherein are fertile Meddowes, pleasant Springs, delightful Streames, and all sorts of beasts of chase and game, and in the middest thereof, a sumptuous house of pleasure.' Although his recollection of the fantastic visions and expressions was distinct, the poet was disturbed on writing the poem, by a man from Porlock. What remains, therefore, is a fragment. The first part goes:

> In Xanadu did Kubla Khan
> A stately pleasure-dome decree:
> Where Alph, the sacred river, ran
> Through caverns measureless to man
> Down to a sunless sea.
> So twice five miles of fertile ground
> With walls and towers were girdled round:
> And there were gardens bright with sinuous rills,
> Where blossomed many an incense-bearing tree;
> And here were forests ancient as the hills,
> Enfolding sunny spots of greenery.[1]

The British poet John Masefield experienced a dream one morning in which was a tall woman, dressed in furs and a tall hat. He sensed the whole of her background in the dream as she looked towards Lincoln's Inn Fields. The dream was very clear and Masefield noted the sun shining, and pigeons pecking for food. As the woman disappeared from the dream, he noticed a poem that was engraved in high relief on an oblong metal plate. The poem seemed to explain the woman's past life, her feelings, and her perceptions that morning. On waking, Masefield wrote down the poem:

The Woman Speaks

> Bitter it is, indeed, in human fate
> When Life's supreme temptation comes too late.
> I had a ten years' schooling, where I won
> Prizes for headache and caparison.
> I married well; I kept a husband warm
> With twenty general years of gentle charm.
> We wandered much, where'er our kind resort,
> But not till Sunday to the Inns of Court.
> So then imagine what a joy to see
> The town's grey, vast and unappeasèd sea
> Suddenly still, and what a hell to learn
> Life might be quiet, could I but return.[2]

Peter Lyons is a London designer who produces some extraordinarily imaginative one-off objects. His many commissions

Fig. 18.
Masks designed by Peter Lyons, who obtains much
inspiration from his dreamlife

include pieces of jewellery, masks (see Fig. 18), head-dresses, chandeliers, puppets, hats and bead-woven apparel. He makes plentiful use of his recalled dream imagery in these various creations. Peter's dreams have always been vivid, and he had developed to the stage of semi-lucidity. He states:

> I love dreaming, and I value my dream-life highly. One of the most enjoyable qualities of dream-life, I find, is its often subtle, elegant, and witty way of characterizing reality, even though it may be completely bizarre. I dip into my dreams for inspiration. I've experienced ravishing music (of my own composition), and gazed on the most magnificent architecture and scenery in my dream world. I can envisage lucid dreaming being used as a marvellously powerful aid to creativity.

Terri Dixon is an artist from Cleethorpes, South Humberside, and is very up-and-coming. She has exhibited widely in galleries and various shows, and her paintings are being bought by the wealthy and famous on an increasing scale. Dream-like scenes have featured in several of her works. Thus a person is seen flying, arms outstretched, above a typical local street-scene. Terri took part in an experiment in which she used a dream machine.

The device was set to the mode of operation where the dreamer is woken immediately at an emotional point in the dream. Terri emerged from many dreams at interesting stages, with unusual imagery present in the dream-scenery. She was able to recreate those scenes from memory. Thus the device greatly increased her 'data base' of visual experience and provided unique images for her to portray.

The dream may provide some marvellous ideas for art, but the practical skills have to exist to externalize the images. In my own dreams I have entered art galleries and seen some exquisite and, so far as I know, original paintings, but I totally lack any artistic ability that could reproduce them adequately. In fact, I recall that last night I saw in a dream a framed portrait of a woman, which was a sort of coloured-line drawing with some colouring-in. It was very unusual, because the economical lines showing the face also merged with the background. The arrangement was beautiful, like a modern *Mona Lisa*. I admired the picture very greatly, but I am afraid it can never be transferred from the dream world to the waking world!

Music is somewhat different. I compose various items of music, and occasionally in dreams wonderful melodies have presented themselves—some of which I have managed to write down on waking. An example is the 'Hail Mary' piece (see Fig. 19). At that time I was working on some religious music and was considering various ideas for that prayer, mostly involving a 'modern' theme. However, in a dream I was in a church and heard a woman sing

Fig. 19.
'Hail Mary'. The tune is based on a hymn, in traditional church style, heard in a dream by the author

a beautiful traditional hymn-type 'Hail Mary'. The word Jesus was emphasized by slow, majestic, moving chords. That is really the only part I could recall on waking. The rest of the piece that I wrote is in a similar style to what I heard. It should best be played on a modern synthesizer, using a good 'strings' sound, and a woman with a warm soprano voice should sing the words.

Psychotherapist Robin Furman has heard many fine tunes in his dreams. He gives this account of one experience:

Fig. 20.
'Dream Theme' by Robin Furman. This music was heard in a dream and written down on waking

I was standing in an opulent salon or drawing-room. In there were a number of antique cabinets filled with rare china. Two elegantly dressed elderly ladies were looking into the cabinets. I recall that they were wearing furs and pearls. A young, rather attractive, girl then entered and after a moment began slowly to ballet-dance about the room. As she twirled round and round, I began to hear a song being sung and then noticed that she was singing as she danced. There was a curious anomaly in that although she was singing her lips did not move, but her mouth remained partly open for the song to issue forth. This singing and dancing lasted long enough for me to remember the melody.

Robin dashed to the piano and wrote down the theme he had just heard. The music is reproduced in Fig. 20.

Lucid potential

The lucid-dream state holds considerable potential for creative people. Because the environment is subject to volitional altera-tion in these dreams, the dreamer may manoeuvre the dream to a situation where original material is experienced. In such a way, a composer, say, might decide in the dream to enter a concert hall and hear a new piece, or a poet might enter a library and look at a poem never before seen, or an architect might gaze upon some spectacular new building. Although in practice there is often some difficulty in setting up conditions for creativity in dreams, enough trial-and-error attempts should establish a suitable dream source of novel perceptions.

Lucid dreams, then, have a major advantage over ordinary dreaming and we can expect that creative people in many fields will seek to tap into this limitless reservoir of ideas in the future—now that this El Dorado had been mapped-out.

At a lesser level, lucid dreams may be enjoyed for their sheer recreational potential. A few minutes of some spectacular, exciting or relaxing unusual experience can have a greatly beneficial psychological effect and can elevate mood the next day, just as the nightmare's effect protrudes into waking life for several hours:

I have lucid dreams of flying—which is very pleasant. I dream I am walking along the street and I have an urge to fly, so I flap my arms and take off. I fly over the buildings and out to sea and I can go anywhere I want. Sometimes when I am flying, I feel so happy and free that I cry. The feeling is so strong and when I have the dream it leaves me feeling happy and contented for a couple of weeks afterwards.

Some people utilize their lucid dreams to practise motor skills. A ballet dancer reported that she improved her style in lucid dreams, and a swimmer developed a more efficient technique in waking life from his dream experience of swimming.

The source of originality

Can dreams create new perceptions? In the last century, L.F.A. Maury considered this matter and concluded:

> The eye, and the ear and the senses in general, have an ability to fuse and construct—relating to the creative power of the imagination. The components used are provided by past-perceived sensations, but their arrangement and method of assembly is original and results in visual images and sounds which are different from those perceived before.[3]

Saint-Denys, in his careful introspections, discovered that the basis of many of his dream scenes was from a specific waking source, such as an engraving, but the dream process was able to animate the picture and continue along some plausible associative pathway.

The amount of recombination of perceptual components is variable on different occasions, so the degree of originality varies. Saint-Denys gave one cautionary tale involving no dream creativity, only a play-back of something once perceived. A musician friend of his heard a piece in a dream and wrote it down on waking. It sounded new to him. Years later, he found the same piece of music in an old collection, but still could not recall where he had heard it first. The same could happen with waking compositions, however. After all, every composition is based on something similar that has been perceived at some time.

Nevertheless, considerable originality does indeed occur in dreams. Saint-Denys described some imagery which he could not possibly have seen in real life before:

> I dreamed I saw a young woman dressed in an old-fashioned way,

who was fooling with some pieces of red-hot metal it seemed without any harm. Whenever she touched them, long protruberences of flame stayed hanging from her fingers; and when she rubbed her hands there was a shower of sparks and a loud bang.

As an example of the alterations to images that results in original pictures, Saint-Denys described facial changes:

> I was looking at myself in a magic mirror, where I saw myself by sequence in a number of different guises: my hair and beard were in several different conditions—youthful and very flawless; then I was fat-faced, yellowing, ill-looking, toothless, several years older. My face passed through these successive alterations and eventually looked so frightening that I awoke with a jump.

Saint Denys accepted the principle that in dreams the imagination can construct new perceptions from material that exists in memory.

It would be of tremendous value to be able to obtain some index of originality in a lucid dream, so that if a seemingly original composition, say, were heard, a test could be made in the dream to indicate its novelty. This might be possible because the 'recombination of perceptual memory elements' factor could well be operating at a particular level during the whole of the dream. A test might be to look at one's dream hands to see how different they are from waking life, or to observe the scenery carefully for 'impossible' images. The more bizarre the imagery, it may be that the creative composition is the more original.

Fear control

Even the simple fact of *knowing* that dream control is feasible can have an extraordinarily beneficial effect in some people who had, prior to that information, suffered from bad dreams in which uncontrolled and terrible things happened. The first case I found was two days after I gave an interview on Radio Merseyside on 26 October 1976. In the interview I described fully my signalling-from-dreams discovery, and discussed the features of lucid dreams – including the ability to control events. A lady in Liverpool wrote the following:

> I listened to you on Radio Merseyside on Tuesday, but never thought

that I would be writing to you. In the evening I tried to explain lucid dreaming to my husband and daughter. Until then, I had never been aware of having a lucid dream. I have vivid dreams and nightmares revolving around me lying in bed sleeping. Thus, on first awakening, it takes a little time to realize that it is only a dream and not reality. However, my last thoughts before going to sleep on Tuesday night were about the interview and I believe the result was a lucid dream.

I was back in my mother-in-law's house (she died in February). Occupying most of the living-room was an extra large coffin, with the lid propped open. Four undertakers dressed in black with long, frightening faces were standing by. In an equivalent situation at any other time, this is the point where I would wake up screaming, but on Tuesday there followed a completely different pattern. Suddenly, I wasn't frightened anymore. I smiled happily and distinctly remember saying, 'It is all right. It is only a dream.' I then laughingly suggested that we moved the coffin lid up and down slowly to make it creak and groan. When I awoke, I recalled it all quite clearly but without fear. I felt that I must write to you because I truly believe that if I had not listened to your interview I would have woken up screaming as usual. I believe that you can really help to allay not only nightmare dreams but the accompanying fears and depression.

'Primitives'

The full potential of dreaming has been harvested for years by several 'primitive' peoples, including the Senoi, the tribe in Malaysia, visited by the American psychologist, Patricia Garfield. Dreams are discussed in detail in that community, and most individuals seem to have developed the ability to dream lucidly—which shows what could also be achieved in the West. The dream world is given equal status to the waking world.

Their society is remarkably free of strife, and it has been suggested that this is largely due to the great influence dreams have in that culture. The Senoi make much use of the creative process in dreaming.

A major technique employed by them is to overcome any hostile spirits in dreams and make them into a force on one's own side. Any aggressive entity in the dream must be approached and subdued, for instance, by calling up powerful reserves of previously overcome spirits. The vanquished spirit is then asked for a gift or trophy—something like a poem or a dance—and this is performed for the community on waking. Sometimes the gift may be information about something that will be of benefit to the individual or the group if it is sought, such as the location of a new food supply.

With the free discussion of dream events throughout the tribe, antagonisms and jealousies are fully analysed and resolutions sought. It is that constant defusing of controversies that perhaps causes the tribe to be so cohesive and peaceful. There must be lessons here for all of us.

Summary

It should be obvious that the dream state, with its infinite capacity to juggle around perceptual memory 'bits' and come up with new images and sounds, could assist the creativity of gifted artists and scientists. For other mortals, the dream state can be a holiday world in which the 'oneironaut' may participate in all manner of recreational activities, from flying to simply gazing in awe at the complexity of the fake imagery in the surrounding scenery. Dream realization can transform bad dreams to happy ones, and so end much misery for chronic sufferers.

The lucid dream state is to be preferred for these features, but ordinary dreams, if observed carefully by a strict regime of note-taking on waking, can also lead to the recognition of interesting and valuable material.

Several allegedly 'primitive' societies have a positive attitude to dreams and utilize them constructively in the personal lives of individuals and for the group. Unfortunately, in the West there is a disdainful attitude to interest in dreams (largely caused by organized religion associating it with sorcery). All the while, though, it would seem that we have unwittingly deprived ourselves of at least a useful and possibly essential means of creativity and problem-solving.

References
1. *The Complete Works of Samuel Taylor Coleridge*. Ed. E.H. Coleridge (1968). Clarendon Press, Oxford.
2. *Poems by John Masefield* (1966). Heinemann, London.
3. Maury, L.F.A. (1861) *Le Sommeil et les Rêves: étude psychologique*, p102.

8

Inside Information

For the student wishing to know more about dreams and dreaming, it is essential to have an understanding of certain unusual phenomena which might be met during his or her development in the art of dreaming. In this chapter, sleep paralysis, false awakenings and other anomalies will be illustrated and discussed. A method (F.A.S.T.) of experimental lucidity induction will be described, and some useful techniques in dream control revealed.

Sleep paralysis

This temporary condition, although not widely experienced, is the result of a quite normal bodily change that happens in dreaming sleep. The person 'wakes' and feels quite unable to move or to make vocalizations. It is like being bound tightly, and gagged. To anyone not comprehending the nature of this condition, it can be frightening because it is as if one is 'trapped in sleep'. Some people even imagine that they must be dead! If struggling is attempted, the situation is exacerbated and exhaustion results. To the sophisticated dreamer, however, the condition is one of great interest, and several fascinating experiments may be conducted during the state.

The following are typical cases from my files:

> I thought I'd died. I tried to signal to my husband to wake me up. I tried to nudge him but I couldn't move. All I wanted to do was to wake up. I tried to make a noise. I thought I did but he said he didn't hear anything. It really worried me.

I am sure that my husband is lying beside me so I shout to him at the top of my voice to help me and dig him ferociously to try to attract his attention. He always insists that I made no sound.

I struggle desperately to wake up fully. I try to attract my wife's attention by making small bodily movements, so that she can wake me, but it always leaves me physically and mentally exhausted.

As I child I often woke up terrified. I thought I was biting and shouting at my mother. When I really woke up she hadn't felt or heard anything. I still experience this thing. I've tried to relax and pray. I'm afraid someone will think I'm dead and I'll be buried alive.

I am totally paralysed and am fully aware of the fact. I know that it will take something outside of myself to awaken me: a touch, a noise.

These subjects were all paralysed and although in some cases they thought they were shouting or making movements, these were illusory.

On some occasions, 'intruders'—some with evil intent—may be hallucinated in the bedroom.

I felt that someone stood behind me with a knife.

I heard footsteps on the stairs. The bedroom door started to open and was creaking. I was laid with my eyes open and I could see the door open but could not move because I was totally paralysed. When I woke up, the door was tightly shut.

I imagined that somebody was laying in bed with me, but I couldn't see them because I was struggling to turn over but couldn't move.

I was lying on my stomach when I felt a hand caressing my back. I was scared and lay still for a while, thinking who could it be. The hands came under my stomach, up my body onto my shoulders and down my back again. I pushed myself up and half turned my body and I could see sitting on my bed a young boy. I thought then I must be dreaming. The youth, of about 18, kept on caressing my back. Then his hand reached out as if to touch my cheek, but I bit his hand. I then lay down again and went back to sleep.

The woman who thought she saw the door opening did not actually have her eyes open, and if the intruders were really present, the response would be much more real. The woman feeling an unknown lad caress her would not realistically just fall back to sleep. They are dreamlike happenings.

What causes sleep paralysis is straightforward. It is the normal bodily paralysis that accompanies Stage REM (dreaming) sleep and which is unexpectedly experienced here in partial waking. In REM there is an active inhibition of the musculature—with some exceptions, such as those muscles of the eyes and those concerned with breathing. Only small bodily twitches are observed during dreaming sleep. Although the person seems to wake up the whole episode is dreamed, but the accompanying paralysis is present and can be felt during the slight rousing.

Sleep paralysis is also known as 'night nurses' paralysis'. Anyone who has a shift-work job and falls asleep when he or she is supposed to be vigilant is likely to experience the condition. There is an element of expectation in that the person knows they should not be asleep, so it is not too surprising that they dream of hearing Matron, say, approaching. In some cases it seems that external sounds are incorporated into the dream, but it is more likely that they are hallucinated.

During my research at Liverpool University, I was often very tired when monitoring the polygraph all night. Sometimes I fell asleep and experienced sleep paralysis. Typically, there was a feeling of being 'bound' and imagining that security guards were chatting just outside the room (which they were not).

Some ghost stories originate from the hallucinatory effects of sleep paralysis. For instance, one young woman reported that she woke and saw the figure of an old woman at the foot of her bed. The girl thought it was a ghost, and found herself totally paralysed. Another person stated that she woke, quite unable to move her body, and became extremely frightened when she noticed the bedclothes rippling supernaturally.

The way to deal with sleep paralysis is simply to realize what it is and not to struggle. REM periods are temporary, so the paralysis will certainly come to an end quite naturally when one proceeds to slow-wave sleep, or wakes. There is no need to worry.

As for any events that seem to be going on around, like the suspected presence of intruders, if you cannot move then you are dreaming and you are therefore hallucinating. Recall what has been written here, about the frequent feature of sleep paralysis— the presence of 'intruders'. If you simply think, 'It's sleep paralysis. I'm dreaming, so I shall ignore what seems to be going on, relax, and go back to sleep,' that will almost certainly work immediately and you will enter an ordinary dream.

However, the state of sleep paralysis affords a marvellous opportunity for experimentation, and these episodes are sought keenly by dream exponents. The condition is unique; it is like a false awakening (see next section), yet one is paralysed, so interaction with others and the environment is not possible. It is an ideal moment at which to attempt an 'out-of-the-body' experience. Since the condition is a dream, a strong command to oneself to 'slip out' or 'roll out' of the body may well succeed, and an incredible experience will ensue. You may walk about your house, like a ghost, and possibly find some amazing differences. OBEs are usually very clear and have a quality somewhat distinct from that of lucid dreams.

There is a medical condition, known as narcolepsy,[1] affecting perhaps 1 person in 100 000 of the population, where sufferers tend to collapse during the day and enter REM sleep immediately. It is very much like sleep paralysis, but there seems to be more awareness of what is actually happening around. The collapse is caused by the muscular inactivity of REM, and may be triggered by emotion—and even laughing.

For anyone greatly troubled by sleep paralysis, a cure is at hand. The sufferer's problem, as the accounts vividly demonstrate, is that there is no way of communicating to the sleeper's partner or anyone else. If someone, or something, could be made aware of the sleeper's distress, the person could be roused properly. The dream machine enables that communication to occur. On becoming aware of being in sleep paralysis, the sufferer simply makes a sequence of rapid breaths, so setting off the device. An incrementing audible alarm will then waken the person properly. Breathing remains under voluntary control and is unaffected by the sleep paralysis of REM sleep.

False awakenings

A false awakening is the convincing illusion of having woken, when one is still actually asleep and dreaming. It is distinct from sleep paralysis, where one seems to waken but is paralysed, in that everything appears perfectly normal and one can 'move' naturally. However, it is all a dream. It probably happens to people very often but, of course, the verisimilitude of the imagery is such that the state is just not recognized for what it really is.

> I am in the bedroom and awake and wish to know the time. I raise my head and try to read the digital clock, but the figures are not comprehensible and are in the wrong order. I turn on the radio, but there is no sound. I try to switch on the light. The switch operates, but the light does not appear. I walk to the bedroom door but that will not open. I then realize that I am dreaming.

A false awakening may come after an unpleasant dream:

> I had just come home from an evening out and was fully clothed, when I heard a noise in my daughter's bedroom. I went to investigate. The room was different, and a man was there wearing a leather headgear with studs on it. He was chained. He went berserk and tried to get free but could not do so, and started crying. I said I could help him get free but as I started to assist him, he struggled wildly again, so I ran from the room. I ran into my own room, jumped on the bed, and my daughter woke up and asked me what was the matter. I told her I had just had a bad dream. She asked what happened, and I pointed to the other bedroom. I looked at the wall as I pointed to it and then ducked in time as a hail of bullets came through the wall. I felt the bullets whiz past my head. 'Phew,' I said to my daughter calmly, 'that was a near thing.' I then turned over onto my left side and woke up. I then realized the whole thing had been a dream!

A false awakening commonly follows on from a lucid dream. In the next case, the false awakening was recognized yet the dreamer explored the environment. She returned to bed using a method tried and tested before by her:

> I woke up, I thought, after having a dream in which a woman was knocking on my bedroom window, with my daughter in her arms. The window is upstairs, so I knew it was impossible, and was lucid. I went to look into my daughter's bedroom, but the room had changed. The carpet was gone and replaced by lino, which I could feel under my bare feet. The room looked distorted, although my bedroom had looked normal. I went downstairs to check things. I felt so wide awake that I could hardly believe I was dreaming. I noticed the pram had been moved, and the kettle had been switched on in the kitchen and was about to boil (I was the only person in the house who could have put it on). In the living-room, all the furniture had been rearranged. I wondered if I should switch off the kettle, but thought whoever put it on would be back soon. I then wanted to get away quickly, because I did not want to meet that person. I closed

my eyes and, concentrating hard, imagined myself back in bed—by thinking of the warm sheets around me. This worked and I was back in bed—this time, really awake.

Celia Green[2] noticed two varieties of false awakening in relation to lucid dreams, and categorized them as Type 1 and Type 2. In Type 1, the person considers some previous dream, lucid or not, and then perhaps may seem to wake up, or wonder whether a dream is still happening. A good example, also cited by Green, is this case from van Eeden:[3]

> In February 1899, I had a lucid dream, in which I made the following experiment. I drew with my finger, moistened by saliva, a wet cross on the palm of my left hand, with the intention of seeing whether it would still be there after waking up. Then I *dreamt* that I woke up and felt the wet cross on my left hand by applying the palm to my cheek. And then a long time afterwards I woke up *really* and knew at once that the hand of my physical body had been lying in a closed position undisturbed on my chest all the while. [Page 447.]

The Type 2 false awakening is one where the dreamer seems to wake normally, but the atmosphere is one of suspense. The feeling of stress, excitement or apprehension may appear after a variable amount of time from 'waking':

Oliver Fox[4] wrote:

> I passed from unremembered dreams and thought I was awake. It was still night, and my room very dark. Although it seemed to me that I was awake, I felt curiously disinclined to move. The atmosphere seemed charged, to be in a 'strained' condition. I had a sense of invisible, intangible powers at work, which caused this feeling as of aerial stress. I became expectant. Certainly something was about to happen. [Page 48.]

False awakenings can occur repeatedly in a few individuals, resulting in great confusion. For example, a nurse, having a short sleep on night-duty, dreamed this:

> I dreamt I was sleeping and had wakened on hearing what I thought was one of the nursing officers. I dived across the room, knocking over tables and chairs. Then I heard voices at the door and the door being locked. I then knew I was dreaming and decided to wake up. What I did not realize was that I 'woke' into another dream, and when I stood up everything was lying on the floor as it was in my first

dream. The door was locked, so I began banging on it and shouting to get out. My relief nurse and another nurse unlocked the door. Shortly afterwards, I really woke up.

Several times I have known that I was dreaming when it was time to get up for work. I have tried to wake myself up, but only succeeded in dreaming that I have woken. This could happen four or five times in a row before I actually wake up properly. I'll know it's still a dream usually because the carpet or the bed-sheets are a different colour, or that something else in the room—say the furniture—is not correct.

It was a lovely morning when I awoke, to get up for school. I got up, washed and changed, had breakfast and waited for the school bus. I was chatting to friends, when there was a bang, and I woke up. I got up, washed, changed, had breakfast, caught the bus, and arrived at school. During registration a boy threw a book which hit me on the head, and I woke up! This time, I got up, washed, etc., got to school, had my lessons and was having break, when I asked a girl to pinch me to see if I was actually dreaming, when my mother woke me up! I rushed to get ready for school, told my friends at school all that had happened, and everything went fine until dinnertime, when the school fire-alarm went off. There was panic, someone stumbled over me, and I hurt my leg. I awoke in bed – it was dark and the clock showed 2 a.m. Was I still asleep? It was not until bedtime the next night that I really knew and believed that I was awake.

Out-of-the-body-experiences (OBEs)

The OBE is an umbrella-term covering many different sorts of phenomena, but having in common the situation where the person seems to be outside his or her body. Some people say they can induce these excursions at will. I monitored three such people in the laboratory and found that they were in fact in light (Stage 1) sleep when it was occurring.

It might be argued that some lucid dreams and false awakenings could be OBEs—it depends on where you find yourself. If, in a lucid dream or false awakening, you are in your bedroom and you look round and see yourself (autoscopy), that is very much like an OBE. It is difficult to pigeon-hole these phenomena.

Ten tests for state-assessment

There are moments in ordinary dreams where the dreamer

pauses to consider whether or not he or she is in fact dreaming. There may be some inconsistency in the dream, or just a 'feeling' that something is not quite right.

If a correct analysis is made of the situation at that 'pre-lucid' point, then dream lucidity is initiated—with all its amazing properties and potentials. Often, though, the opportunity is missed, because everything may look correct and critical thought is not operating very effectively at the time. Nevertheless, despite the superficial accuracy of the dream scenery, there are certain detectable peculiarities in dreaming, so that if the dreamer employs a standard set of tests to conduct routinely at such moments the true state can be ascertained more frequently.

The question as to whether one is dreaming or not also arises in the extraordinary condition where the dreamer believes, erroneously, that waking has occurred. In these false awakenings, a perfect reproduction of the bedroom may be presented. Unless tests are performed, the dreamer might have no inkling that the experience was a dream.

The following tests are meant to assist in distinguishing the dreaming state from wakefulness. I published them some years ago, and they are based on my research experience. The tests should be committed to memory, and even practised in the waking state, so that they spring readily to mind when required. The dedicated dream enthusiast might wish to perform a test whenever waking appears to have happened, so that any false awakenings are recognized immediately. Any incongruity noticed in the environment as a consequence of performing a test should instigate lucidity.

1 Switch on an electric light in the dream scenery. If it does not work, or there is a malfunction *of any kind*, or light switches cannot be found where they should exist, suspect very strongly that you are dreaming. The same applies for any other electrical appliance.

2 Attempt to 'float' in mid-air, or fly. Any success, of course, is proof of dreaming.

3 Jump off an object, such as a chair. If you descend slowly, then you know you are dreaming.

4 Look carefully at your surroundings. Is there anything there which should not be present?

5 Look at your body (e.g. hands, arms, feet) and your clothes. Is it *your* body, and are the clothes yours in wakefulness?

6 Look out of a window. Is the environment accurate? Is the season correct, and is the light-level right for the time?
7 Attempt to alter a detail in the scenery, or make something happen by will-power.
8 Attempt to push your hand through solid-looking objects.
9 Pinch your skin. Is the texture as it should be?
10 Look in a mirror. Is there some alteration to your face?

The 'F.A.S.T.' technique

Having conducted very many sleep experiments over several years, one of the things I noticed was the fairly high number of reports of false awakenings from subjects in the sleep-lab. Sometimes, a noise, say, seemed to precipitate the dream of being awake in a realistic reproduction of the sleep-lab, but often a dream of sleep-interruption occurred spontaneously. These false awakenings tended to happen when a sleep disturbance was to be expected by the subject—for instance, if the subject was told that he or she would be woken for a dream report at some time in the night. The sleeping mind becomes rather fixated on the coming event, so it is not surprising that false awakenings can be prompted in that situation of high anticipation.

The most common account is that an experimenter enters the bedroom and engages in conversation with the subjects, or perhaps adjusts the electrodes. All the while, though, the chart record shows that the subject is in undisturbed REM sleep.

Expectation can produce strong effects in people. There is the well-known phenomenon of the 'placebo effect', where perhaps half the patients given a 'drug' (which is in fact an inert substance) will report that it produced an alleviation of symptoms. In an experiment that I ran at Liverpool University, 70 per cent of the subjects reported that they had dreamed of topics suggested to them before sleep.[5]

The thought occurred to me that the false awakening state is half-way to lucidity, in a sense, so perhaps it might be employed in some fashion to leap-frog to dream-awareness. A two-stage technique came to mind, involving the production of false awakenings and the subsequent realization of dreaming.

The first part of the F.A.S.T. technique is designed to produce, or encourage, false awakenings, by introducing a situation of strong expectation. In practical terms, it is suggested that an assistant simply enters your bedroom, says a few words, perhaps prods you, and then leaves. You should not attempt to respond in any way. This procedure should be repeated intermittently— say, every half-hour—over the last two hours of the night's sleep (when REM is plentiful), or throughout a day-time sleep. On being disturbed, you may:

(a) wake up properly;
(b) not awaken—in SWS or REM sleep;
(c) partially waken in SWS and return to that state;
(d) partially waken in REM, and return to REM.

A false awakening could happen in (d). More important perhaps is that at any time the expectation might produce a dream of being disturbed—in the absence of any real interruption.

The second stage of the technique concerns the detection by the subject of a false awakening, so initiating dream lucidity. Thus, on each occasion that you think you have woken—no matter how sure you are—you must perform certain tests of state-assessment. A list of tests has already been given, but for the special situation of this experiment, the following are suggested:

1   Do not speak or make any gross body movements, but simply try to move a hand or foot. If it feels unusually heavy, or you are unable to move it, suspect that you are dreaming. It may be sleep paralysis.
2   If you feel sure that you can move your body, keep generally still, but attempt, say, to push your hand through the bed.
3   Listen carefully to what is going on around you. Are the sounds appropriate, or incongruous and perhaps distorted?
4   If there is a light around you, should that be so? If you are viewing a bedroom scene, are the details correct?
5   Attempt to float up slowly from the bed, or even to sink through the bed.
6   'Will' yourself to another room in the house.

Any unusual results from these tests should initiate dream lucidity, or an out-of-the-body experience. Once you are 'up', a further state-test is to try to switch on an electric light. Difficulties are usually encountered.

On waking, check with your assistant as to whether the disturbances actually happened, and go over the details. Confer over precisely what was said by the assistant during the disturb-ances, how many prods were given, whether the light was switched on, etc. You may have missed a false awakening.

The F.A.S.T. method may have some success with a minority of people, particularly those who frequently recall their dreams and question their state in dreams. The great range of differences between people in their psychological responses to such situa-tions makes it impossible to predict its efficiency for individuals. Nevertheless, if the method is practised, its effects may be more reliably produced. Certainly, it helps focus one's attention on dreams and dreaming in an interesting way. As with several psychological effects, the results are likely to be more successful if some further novelty is introduced, so that, say, a different assistant is employed or the bedroom is changed. The technique is an entertaining one to attempt at 'dream-weekend' seminars!

One person told me:

> I tried your technique a few times without success, with my girl-friend as the assistant. However, when another friend acted as the 'disturber' on one occasion, I dreamed at one point that I was chatting to him about the experiment. Everything was realistic, but I suddenly realized that the bedroom was not accurate. Its shape was wrong. I said I was dreaming and got excited. I tried the light switch, but it did not operate. This gave me further proof of dreaming. I looked carefully at the intricate detail in objects in the scenery, and then woke up.

There are variations on the same theme which dream-enthusiasts may like to try. For instance, instead of having someone physically disturb the subject, the subject could be telephoned by someone at the corresponding times. The phone should just ring two or three times, and the subject should not answer the call. One of the things to look out for in the subject in this condition is any 'fault' that occurs with the phone. Electrical gadgets in dreams are frequently 'out of order'.

Serial lucid dreams

There is a variety of lucid dream that some people report where, on each occasion, the dream carries on from where it previously left off. It is rather like having another dream-world existence, which shows consistencies and coherence as in waking life. The

story unfolds in serial fashion, but the dream has full consciousness and volition.

> Each night in sleep I experience a rushing sound, have the sensation
> of going through a tunnel, and find myself transported in a dream to
> another planet somewhere. I am greeted by a woman – the same
> woman each time – and she shows me over the city. Everything is
> futuristic and there is strange, imaginative architecture. For example,
> one massive structure has two large globes one on top of the other,
> on a tower. I ask questions and receive answers, and I choose where
> I want to go. All the while I know I am dreaming.

Location-changing

There are lots of ways of establishing a new location in lucid
dreams. Among the gradual ways are: walking to another place,
taking some form of dream-transport, and 'flying' using your
arms. Always, you must have fixed in your mind where you want
to be; this seems to programme the dream-producing process.

A favourite 'instant' mode of travel is closing or covering the
(dream) eyes and willing yourself to a new place. It is best,
though, to experiment in lucid dreams and find out the best
method for you. Perhaps, say, a little ritual—such as spinning
round—linked with the 'target' thought, might work routinely for
you.

Conjuring people and objects

The ability to 'call' specific persons into the lucid dream varies
between individuals. In some, simply thinking of that person will
result in a visitation from them. Devious measures may also be
employed—for instance, 'willing' someone to be behind a closed
door, and then opening it. You may also attempt to 'visit' the
person yourself, by dream-travel.

Similarly, objects can sometimes be conjured up rapidly, but
often the dream has to be manoeuvred in some way so as to bring
about the wished-for effect; thus you could 'will' yourself to find
an object in a drawer.

Sound-facilitation technique

For lucid dreamers who experience problems in trying to

produce a rapid change of location in dreams, it may be facilitated by imagining any sounds associated with the place you wish to visit. One subject, for instance, stated that she had always in the past walked over to a corner, horizon, or any area that was currently out of view, knowing that when she reached that place it would be as she had chosen. She then began to use the method of scene-change involving closing her (dream) eyes, wishing to be at a specific location, then opening her (dream) eyes. The effect was greatly enhanced by first imagining the *sound* of the intended new scene, e.g. hearing waves breaking on a beach. Other subjects have reported similar findings.

Deliberate waking

There are certain circumstances when the lucid dreamer wishes to waken immediately, for example, to note down something important about the lucid dream. Here, too, people vary as to how easily this can be accomplished. A deliberate effort may work easily. On the other hand, some subterfuge may have to be resorted to, so as to gain release from the grasp of REM sleep:

> When I want to wake up, I simply make an effort to open my eyes. It always works.

> In my lucid dreams, I can awaken myself by doing certain things. One of them is to jump into some water! I know that in a moment I shall be wide awake.

> I found, by experimentation, that the only way I could exit a lucid dream quickly, to wakefulness, was to stand on my toes and press on the floor very hard. I don't know how or why this works, but it happens.

Whatever the method used, one should always question one's state when apparently waking from a lucid dream. False awakenings can easily follow, without the dreamer realizing.

Incidentally, waking from a lucid dream—or false awakening—may be preceded in some people by strange noises, such as a 'buzzing' sound.

> I have been dreaming lucidly, but then there is a buzzing in my head. I wake up into another dream with a (dream) bee buzzing around. I then wake up properly.

Further dream-control ideas

Objects may be conjured up in the lucid dream and utilized to assist in the process of dream control. Thus, if one is 'flying' against a 'head wind', a motorized unit might be produced to overcome the resistance! If possible, the fact that the dream proceeds by visual and verbal associations should be remembered, so that if the dream scenery is that of a jungle, and a snake is observed, the thought that it looks like a winding road might transform the scene accordingly.

It is important to maintain full mastery of the dream. Various 'weapons systems' may be created and employed in the dream if necessary against any threatening dream characters. One effective reported method is to aim your dream fingers at the 'foe' and 'zap' him, using laser-type beams emanating from the fingertips.

The frequent lucid dreamer should, systematically and intelligently, discover how to operate in the dream world to the maximum advantage and efficiency. Keeping a dream diary, constantly conducting experiments, and assessing the feedback information, will greatly enhance one's prowess in the art of dreaming.

References

1.   Roth, B. (1973) Narcolepsy and hypersomnia. In *Sleep Disorders, Diagnosis and Treatment*, eds. Williams, R.L., Karacan, I. & Frazier, S.H.J. Wiley & Sons, New York, pp29–60.
2.   Green, C. (1968) *Lucid Dreams*. Institute of Psychophysical Research, Oxford.
3.   Van Eeden, F. (1913) A study of dreams. *Proceedings of the Society for Psychical Research*, **XXVI** (Part LXVII), 431–61.
4.   Fox, O. (1962) *Astral Projection*. University Books, Inc. New York.
5.   Wagstaff, G., Hearne, K.M.T., & Jackson, B. (1980) Post-hypnotically suggested dreams and the sleep cycle: an experimental re-evaluation. *IRCS Medical Science: Nervous system; Physiology; Psychology*, **8**, 240–41.

9

Dreams–The Changing Image

What are the major ideas that have been proposed to explain dreams? In this chapter, ancient and recent ideas will be described and discussed. The range of theories is considerable, indicating the depth of the great mystery. The remarkable state of 'lucid' dreaming—where consciousness appears in a 'fake' world—leads, in conjunction with other findings, to the amazing possibility that what we take to be waking reality is in fact a convincing but similarly dreamlike experience. This topic will also be examined in detail.

Ancient notions

A common view in ancient societies was that the dream constituted a mode of communication between different parts of this world, with the afterlife, and with the gods. The Assyrians and Babylonians built temples dedicated to dream deities, and several clay-table writings have been found giving details of their ideas on dream interpretation. They understood that verbal puns could appear in dreams.

Papyri have survived from the time of the ancient Egyptians concerning their particular beliefs on dreams. They practised a ritual know as 'dream incubation', whereby the incubant would, after various cleansing behaviours, sleep in a temple, or Serapeum (Serapis was the god of dreams). In the highly magical and reverential atmosphere of the temple, it was not surprising that powerful and apparently significant dreams would ensue. The content was reported to priests who were skilled at interpretation. It might be an answer on how to cure an illness, say, or the dream might foretell future events in the incubant's life. The interpreters noted that dreams often represented opposites, thus to dream of a death could refer to an imminent birth.

In early Chinese society, the soul, or 'hun', was supposed to wander from the body at night and in that free condition it could contact the dead. The different types of dream were carefully categorized, and it was thought that disturbing dreams resulted from an imbalance of the opposite Yin and Yang energies. In this culture, too, the concept of opposites in dream interpretation existed. They recognized that external stimuli could be incorporated into dreams.

Early Indian beliefs were also recorded, in a book of wisdom—the *Atharva Veda*. Aggressive dreams were generally viewed as masterful and positive. Concerning precognitive dreams, it was thought that the later into the sleep period the dream occurred, the sooner the precognized events would come to pass. If a series of dreams happened, only the last should be interpreted—suggesting some form of psychological refining process. These people also linked the dream to the dreamer's temperament, so introducing a new variable into the interpretation.

There were several different ideas on dreams in ancient Greece. Dream incubation was common then, often in relation to seeking healing. The Greeks recognized 'true' and 'false' dreams. Homer stated that true dreams came through the gate of horn, while false ones arrived via the gate of ivory (based on a Greek pun). Symbolism was recognized in dreams, so that to dream of floods indicated an excess of blood—which was itself believed to result in an imbalance of temperament. Imminent illnesses might be presaged by 'prodromic' dreams; thus an incipient problem with the lungs might be indicated by dreams of fire.

Roman beliefs were rather similar to those of the Greeks. An immensely informative work on dream interpretation, *Oneirocritica* by Artemidorus (c. AD 200), has survived. It drew upon much early information and reflected the state of the art at that time. Dream interpretation was a complex process, in which certain points had to be ascertained initially because they might influence the dream, such as the dreamer's occupation, name, the conditions under which the dream occurred, and so on. Associations were obtained and any puns observed. Symbolism was accepted quite naturally, including sexual forms. Clearly, much accumulated observation and knowledge from several civilizations over millennia had crystallized into the Roman art of dream interpretation.

Unfortunately, in Western societies, interest in dreams was somewhat suppressed during the Middle Ages by official Christianity linking dream divination with sorcery. This heavy-handed behaviour effectively halted any progress in understanding dreams for centuries.

More recent ideas

In the nineteenth century, several writers were propounding their ideas about dreams, based on their observations. They considered certain relevant matters that naturally sought answers. It was recognized that the material of dreams was based on memories, often long-forgotten at a conscious level. External and internal physiological stimuli were believed to affect the dream content, and some of the 'typical' dreams—such as of flying—were thought to be caused by the sensation of breathing during dreaming.

There was disagreement over how important psychological factors were in influencing dreams. Certainly, 'day residues'—events that happened during the previous day—could be observed in dreams, but no direct links could be seen by most writers between dreams and the individual's psychology.

The rapid evaporation from memory of dreams was tackled by several writers: the lack of order in dreams made them unmemorable; sensory input on waking swamped the dream memories; there was a general disinterest in dreams, so they were not recalled; and so on.

The presence of associations in dreams was apparent, so that the dream might progress along a series of verbal links, and it was widely agreed that wishes were often expressed in dreams.

As to theories about dreaming, most thought the dream to be rather useless, merely reflecting the action of a fatigued brain operating at an inefficient level. Robert (1866)[1] actually proposed that the dream has a function, which is to excrete useless thoughts. Delage (1891)[1] noted that we do not dream of significant events of the day, and thought that they had not yet been physically adjusted. He also believed that strong impressions which had been accidentally repressed were the subject of dreams. The function of dreams, to him, was to resolve psychological tensions.

Scherner (1861)[1] made some interesting and forthright comments about dreams. He believed that the brain's central control is lacking in dreams, so that fantasy dominates the situation. It builds on waking memories and has to depict thoughts in symbols. The material is largely derived from sensory stimuli, but this material is subservient to the fantasies. The body might be represented symbolically by a house, the penis by a clarinet, pubic hair by fur, and a vagina by a slippery footpath. Scherner could not, however, ascribe a useful function to the dream.

Freud's ideas[1] were built on those of earlier writers, but his dream theory was closely associated with his conceptualization of personality which involves a tripartite structure: the unconscious id, seeking gratification of basic (primary) instincts, especially sex and aggression; the conscious ego, in contact with the real world and aware of society's restraints; and the super-ego, which reminds the person how one ought to behave. In sleep the ego is absent, so the id obtains vicarious gratification via dreams. Freud considered the dream to be the royal road to the knowledge of the unconscious in mental life.

Freud stated that dreams have a meaning and that they are wish-fulfilments. Those were ancient ideas, but he added the notion that dreams represent disguised wishes. Another assertion was that dreams guard (maintain) sleep. Dealing with this latter point first, he believed that the organism basically seeks inactivity and so the function of dreams was to divert the irritable wishes of the id by allowing illusory satisfaction. In that way the organism need not rouse and expend energy.

In order that the ego and super-ego should not be shocked by a direct display of gratification of blatant sexual wishes, the dream had to achieve this via symbolic subterfuge. Therefore a discrepancy exists between the reported dream (manifest content) and the underlying, lascivious, dream thoughts (latent content). The Freudian analyst interprets the dream by tracing the antecedents by a process of free association. People have different personal associations, so no single interpretation can be applied to everyone, but certain universal symbols can have specific meanings, such as the sexual symbolism. Opposites, or reversals, were part of the disguise process in dreams.

Apart from symbolization, other dream-work mechanisms are: condensation, where different wishes combine and form peculiar composites, such a person having the characteristics of two or more separate people; dramatization, or representation, where ideas are presented in images and is like a theatrical performance; and displacement or transference, where important pieces are transferred to some seemingly unimportant element.

Dreams arise, he asserted, either as a direct, suppressed instinctual impulse from the id, or a conscious (ego) desire persisting from the day. The basic, repressed dream thoughts are transformed into acceptable images by the dream-work mechanism, which seeks to evade a hypothetical censor—the super-ego. A process of 'secondary elaboration' or revision, whereby the person tries to make sense of the strange symbolism and associations, may cause further distortion, in reporting.

Freud had great difficulty explaining away anxiety dreams as wish-fulfilments. He pleaded that the dream-work may have been incompetent so that direct latent material intruded, or that the fulfilment of the wish in itself provoked anxiety, or that the censor was overpowered by strong id forces.

Many criticisms have been made of Freudian dream theory. At a very basic level, the philosopher Karl Popper[2] considered that psychoanalytic theory, including dream theory, was a myth— that it was too easily verifiable but not readily falsifiable. Eysenck[3] thought Freudian views unscientific since they are based on unverifiable metapsychological propositions. Certainly, by today's practices, Freud's methods were unscientific.

A great amount of what Freud wrote about dreams had already been stated. He pieced together disparate findings and attempted to link them into a unified theory. Many of the elements probably have some truth in them, such as symbolization and wish-fulfilment, since they have been observed over many generations and in several different cultures. Some studies have shown that symbolization occurs in certain situations in waking life, but to test such a feature and then claim that it supports Freudian theory would be invalid. The overall metapsychology could be wrong. For instance, his claim that symbols disguise repressed sexual wishes could be true, but it could also simply reflect a primitive visual-symbolic 'mentation' in dreams, with no ulterior motive. Freud's understanding of the nervous system was also based on an erroneous 'hydraulic' model, very different from today's ideas.

The close link, obvious to all men, between erections and dreaming seems to indicate a direct link, but in modern sleep-lab studies it has been discovered that the erection cycle can apparently be shifted out of phase with the REM sleep cycle, suggesting that it is a separate physiological arousal not governed by dream mentation.[4]

Thus, while Freud's assertions are bold and superficially compelling, serious doubts are raised on closer examination.

Jung[5] disagreed with the emphasis on sexuality in Freud's approach to dreams, and broke away from his influence. Jung saw the psyche as a self-regulating system, with an energy that can exchange between two opposing extremes of personality, known as the opposites. As we progress in life, these opposing facets of personality become more reconciled, in a process Jung termed individuation. According to Jung, the unconscious might be very different from the conscious persona.

Whereas the unconscious, to Freud, was a backward-looking area of repressed material, Jung envisaged it as a forward-looking, positive feature of the psyche. The way in which it communicated with consciousness was through dreams and other forms of imagery. Jung believed that the dream contains an important message for the dreamer. Its function is to point out any errors in one's personal development, such as becoming too extreme in some personality characteristic. Thus, an over-righteous person might have dreams of a criminal or obscene nature.

In analysis the dream itself is considered rather than remote associative material. Should the dream recur, it indicates that the message has not been properly understood by the dreamer. The analyst attempts to centre any associations on the dream, in a process known as amplification.

Apart from the compensatory characteristic, dreams also look into anticipated future behaviour and events, as if to rehearse, and so are prospective.

There have been some experiments to test Jungian theory. Concerning the major function of dreams as being compensatory, the hypothesis can be deduced that introverted persons should have extroverted dreams, and vice versa. The results have not supported Jung's idea of compensation. In one study, as an example, Domino (1976)[6] collected dream reports from 62 subjects, which were rated on 15 personality dimensions and compared with scores on the same dimension from the subjects. The scores showed that the personality characteristics of the dream person matched those of each dreamer when awake—a finding not in keeping with the Jungian view.

Some modern theories attempt to explain the existence of REM sleep, associated with dreaming, and disregard any psychological significance about dreams. Among some of these widely discrepant theories, we have the following notions: that REM sleep occurs periodically to clear toxins (Dement, 1964);[7] serves to restore the neuromusculature necessary for binocular vision (Berger, 1969);[8] occurs periodically to stimulate the cortex, as SWS may be harmful (Ephron and Carrington, 1966);[9] is a left-over from its function to stimulate the foetus *in utero* (Dement and Fisher, 1963).[10] As it turns out, REM sleep is not actually essential in adults. Some anti-depressant drugs completely abolish REM sleep while they are being used, yet no apparent deleterious effects have been noticed in these patients.

Evans and Newman (1964),[11] treading on the dangerous ground of superficial analogy, proposed that dreams serve as a memory filter, rejecting redundant memories and responses. A similar process happens in computers from time to time, when programs are updated. Redundant material is removed 'off line' in the interests of efficiency. What is perceived in dreams is simply chunks of reorganized data being run through. The theory appeared when it seemed that a 'need to dream' existed. That view has not prevailed, and consequently the theory has been left high and dry.

Some writers and theorists have concentrated on the psychological aspects of dreams.

Adler (1958)[12] proposed a different theory from that of Freud. He believed that sleeping and waking thoughts were similar, but that those in sleep were deficient. Adler therefore believed that both consciousness and the unconscious determined dreams. Sex and aggression no more affect dreams than they do waking existence. He saw symbols not as disguises but as simple representations.

Hall (1954)[13] collected 10,000 samples of dream accounts and broke them down to look at basic things such as settings, and people constituting the dream characters. The most frequent settings were: part of a building (24%); a conveyance (13%); a whole building (11%); a place of recreation (10%); street or road (9%); shop (4%); classroom (4%); office or factory (1%); miscellaneous (14%). In the first named setting, the most common rooms in the dreams were, in order, the living room, bedroom, kitchen, stairway, and basement. Hall found that bizarre and unfamiliar settings are not frequent.

In broad terms, Hall found that dreams are for the most part commonplace and the dream characters tend to reflect the types of people seen and interacted with in waking life. People tend to travel about more in dreams and indulge in recreation. Most reported emotions were unpleasant, though dreamers judged dreams more often pleasant than unpleasant. Hall noted that 29 per cent of the accounts were of dreams in colour, but these dreams seemed not to possess any special characteristics.

In modern dream interpretation, dogmatic assertions have been abandoned and a common-sense attitude prevails. For example, Faraday (1972,[14] 1974[15]) advises that firstly the dream should be taken literally, in case it is a warning, and it should then be taken as a meaningful metaphor—the feelings in the dream are a good clue to the topic. Faraday recognizes three separate types of dream: those giving information about the outside world; those representing subjective attitudes to the external world; and those providing an expression of our feelings about our inner world. Group co-operation is preferable in dream analysis, so that a therapist's views are not imposed on the dreamer.

What can we conclude about dreams from the perspective of the present day? Perhaps the most significant fact we have to face is that, almost certainly, dreaming is not essential in adults. There is no unstoppable 'need to dream'. That sobering point is, of course, a great put-down to many psychological theories and to those theories attempting to ascribe some essential physiological function to REM sleep. That does not, however, mean that dreams are useless; we have seen that dreams hold the most enormous potential for creative and recreational purposes.

The motivating assumption behind Freudian and Jungian dream theories has been that the bizarre features are some kind of disguise. The recent findings with lucid dreaming suggest a simpler scheme of things. Let us consider firstly the 'light-switch effect' (pages 66–69), which points to a ceiling limit on imagery 'brightness' at any particular moment. Probably several other basic limitations exist. An autonomous dream-producing process would appear to operate which has to maintain the dream within those restrictions. Think too of the scene-shift effect (pages 69–72) where the transformation seems to proceed by a 'law of least effort', making use of as little new material as possible. This visual-associative progression at scene-shifts and elsewhere is also accompanied by a constantly running verbal-associative stream.

Consciousness in dreams does not arise simply as a result of cortical stimulation; it is present already. A person woken from an ordinary dream reports having been aware of events *at the time*. It seems, rather, that what happens at lucidity is that long-term memory of one's identity is reconnected (being normally absent in sleep), so abolishing the disorientation and uncritical thinking characteristics of ordinary dreaming.

The 'grinding to a halt' phenomenon (Chapter 4) also tells us things about the dream system. It suggests an internal 'TV screen' and 'video tape' producing unit, the former concerned with the quality of imagery and the latter with the dream material. The system has a feedback loop, so that thoughts can affect, or 'will' the 'imagery compiler' along certain pathways.

On the other hand, such a system cannot be essential, say, to psychological well-being, because congenitally blind persons cope without having visual memories on which to base visual dreams.

In that case, this universally present system must, presumably, have an important function in foetal development. With little or no visual input to provide a visual data bank, innate visual material is probably 'played'—possibly to assist the development of visual perception. The innate visual material may, for instance, consist of intricate patterns and shapes, and some of the objects to which babies respond—such as pairs of eyes, and the 'visual cliff'.[16] This innate foetal imagery may cease around birth.

All in all, then, the latest information reveals that in REM sleep:

1   imagery is manufactured and presented to an internal observer;
2   the production of visual imagery is not a process that can be inhibited;
3   physiological factors control the 'TV screen', i.e. its 'brightness', 'colour', etc.;
4   the dream material is based on memory data, and is compiled along associative verbal and visual pathways by a 'law of least effort';
5   the material is woven into a convincing story acceptable to the level of logic operating at the time, and in a sense 'fools' the dreamer:
6   the process is probably based on a system that is important for the foetus, in developing visual perception, but is not essential after birth;
7   the dream state may be utilized, especially in lucid dreaming, for recreation and creativity.

In these conditions, it is not surprising that bizarre imagery sometimes appears—not from 'repression', but as a result of limitations in the system. The dream is in fact having to cope with some difficult production problems while maintaining its flow by associations.

Life as a 'dream'

Anyone who has experienced a fully lucid dream, and especially a convincing false awakening, cannot help but consider the possibility that wakefulness itself is some kind of 'dream'. The word dream is not quite appropriate because it implies a later waking condition, so let us say some kind of 'mental imagery'. Does the physical universe really exist, or is it an illusion created in the non-physical mind of each of us?

In a lucid dream, everything can appear to be absolutely solid and realistic. Things happen spontaneously, and interactions between people are as in 'real life'. The dream world has its own consistent features. In some people, each time they return to a lucid dream, the events proceed from where they left off. The situation is realized to be distinct from wakefulness, and artificial, but who can be so bold as to say that waking life is definitely not a form of mental imagery? If we question the existence of the 'real world', then we might actually achieve a higher state of insight—that of 'wakefulness lucidity'.

The idea is not new. The ancient Chinese sage Chuang Tzu stated:[17]

> While men are dreaming they do not perceive that it is a dream. Some will even have a dream within a dream. And so when the great awakening comes upon us, shall we know this life to be a great dream. Fools believe themselves to be awake now!

In the West, non-materialism has been frowned upon. The philosopher George Berkeley,[18] though, accepted a physical world but viewed it as a product of an ultimate non-physical reality in God's scheme. But, perhaps all, even now, is pure imagery.

The dream, while it lasts, is the 'real world', but just as there are flaws in the dream world that make us question whether we are dreaming, and thus become dream-lucid, are there flaws in the waking world that would indicate that this too is illusory? The answer is that indeed there are many such pointers, if only we saw them as such.

The great multiplicity of phenomena that constitute the subject matter of parapsychology present us with vast numbers of cases that simply cannot possibly fit into the world as currently conceptualized by mankind.

Throughout recorded history there have been countless reports of such phenomena: psychokinesis (mind over matter); telepathy (mind reading); clairvoyance (remote viewing); poltergeists; premonitions; and many others.[19]

Cases of premonition or precognition are completely incompatible with standard realism, the philosophical opinion in vogue at this time. Yet witnessed, reliable accounts are embarrassingly prevalent in the population.[20] Attempts to explain them away are simply not convincing.

'Percipients' are not so rare either. When I began to investigate the topic of premonitions, following a curious, apparently precognitive incident that happened to me, the first person I asked, a friend, as to whether he knew anyone who had experienced a premonition, told me of his niece who had an incredible forewarning of the Flixborough disaster. I looked into the case thoroughly, and published it as a scientific paper.[21]

Some philosophers, accepting the parapsychological evidence, have expressed disquiet with current thinking. The Oxford philosopher H.H. Price write, in 1949:

> We must conclude, I think, that there is no room for telepathy in a Materialistic universe. Telepathy is something which ought not to happen at all if the Materialistic theory were true. But it does happen. So there must be something seriously wrong with the Materialistic theory, however numerous and imposing the normal facts which support it may be.[22]

The proponents of official science find such views alarming, provocative, and subversive because they undermine its materialistic posture. They refuse to countenance the accumulating evidence of parapsychology–a behaviour remarkably unscientific for so-called science. Of course, if we do all share in a Mind World or Great Illusion, it would mean that science is simply discovering the rules of operation of that scheme.

Are there any testable hypotheses for the existence of a Mind

World? There are actually some possible consequences that suggest themselves. One is that if the extent of the progress of the Great Dream is here and now, then we shall never be able to make contact with alien species more advanced than ourselves, because the dream has not yet reached such a time. Aliens might be at the same level of advancement or be more primitive, but never superior. That is the view which would be at odds with current materialistic science, which assumes that there must be many alien civilizations in space—many of which are millions of years ahead of us. But where are they? Why the great silence?

Another idea the Dream World concept suggests is that we shall never quite be able to reach an understanding of the nature of matter at a sub-atomic level. The Great Illusion will always introduce something to protect its essential deceit.

The Great Illusion viewpoint is also an accepting of the various mysterious religious manifestations and beliefs—miracles, prophets, saviours, and so on. As for an afterlife, one simply enters the next Illusion, just as this episode of life on earth has followed 'termination' in some other existence. While mind-boggling and possibly disturbing to many Westerners, such ideas are perfectly usual in the Orient. Science is too arrogant. Eventually, it may well have to subserve the philosophy of a Dream World.

Conclusions

The investigation of dreams has in fact devalued this state from the point of view of, say, a Freudian or Jungian. Dreams seem to have no essential function in adults, although REM sleep is probably important in the foetus. Nevertheless, all the marvellous potential of dreams is available for exploitation, and the dream machine, with its capacity to increase dream recall, is a very useful modern tool to assist people wishing to learn the art of dreaming. The dream machine may be used to awaken the dreamer in order to recall what was being dreamed (otherwise it would not have entered memory). The unit may also be employed, in various parapsychological experiments, to take advantage of the apparently conducive state of REM sleep to certain psi phenomena. If lucidity can be achieved, via the 'lucidity-induction' mode, then the ultimate state will have been reached in which virtually anything may be willed to happen. In

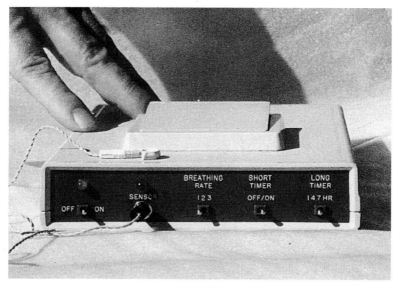

Fig. 21.
The latest model of the dream machine

addition, the novelty of the internal universe may provide much inspiration and material for creative persons.

Dreams are cultivated successfully and positively in some so-called 'primitive' societies. It is something we have to rediscover in the West.

Finally, there are indications that waking life is itself a period of mental imagery, and that the physical universe is a Great Illusion. Several clues exist in the environment to suggest that this is the case. The lucid dreamer is particularly able to comprehend this viewpoint, visiting places in dreams with the full realization of their artificial nature. Perhaps the nursery rhyme said it all:

> Row, row, row the boat
> Gently down the stream,
> Merrily, merrily, merrily, merrily
> Life is but a dream.

References

1. Freud, Sigmund (1961; orig. 1900) *The Interpretation of Dreams.* George Allen and Unwin, London.

2. Popper, K. (1959) *The Logic of Scientific Discovery*. Basic Books, New York.
3. Eysenck, H.J. (1953) *Uses and Abuses of Psychology*. Harmondsworth Penguin, London.
4. Karacan, I., Goodenough, D.R., Shapiro, A., & Starker, S. (1966) Erection cycle during sleep in relation to dream anxiety. *Archives of General Psychiatry*, **15**, 183-9.
5. Fordham, F. (1953) *An Introduction to Jung's Psychology*. Pelican Books, London.
6. Domino, G. (1976) Compensatory aspects of dreams: an empirical test of Jung's theory. *Journal of Personality and Social Psychology*, **34**, 658-62.
7. Dement, W.C. (1964) Experimental dream studies. In *Science and Psychoanalysis, Scientific Proceedings of the Academy of Psychoanalysis*, ed. J. Maserman, **7**, 129-62.
8. Berger, R.J. (1969) Oculomotor control: a possible function of REM sleep. *Psychological Review*, **76**, 144-64.
9. Ephron, H.S. & Carrington, P. (1966) Rapid eye movement sleep and cortical homeostasis. *Psychological Review*, **73**, 500-526.
10. Dement, W.C. & Fisher, C. (1963) Experimental interference with the sleep cycle. *Canadian Psychiatric Association Journal*, **8**, 400-405.
11. Evans, C.R. & Newman, E.A. (1964) Dreaming: an analogy from computers. *New Scientist*, **24**, 577-9.
12. Adler, A. (1958) *What Life Should Mean to You*. Capricorn, New York.
13. Hall, C.S. (1953) *The Meaning of Dreams*. Harper & Row, New York.
14. Faraday, A. (1972) *Dream Power*, Hodder & Stoughton, London.
15. Faraday, A. (1974) *The Dream Game*, Harper & Row, New York.
16. Gibson, E.J. & Walk, R.D. (1960) The visual cliff. *Scientific American*, **202**, 64-71.
17. Giles, H.A. (1926) *Chuang Tzu: Taoist philosopher*. Allen & Unwin, London, p46.
18. Warnock, G.J. (1982) *Berkeley*. Basil Blackwell, Oxford.
19. Dodds, E.R. (1971) Supernormal phenomena in classical antiquity. *Proceedings of the Society for Psychical Research*, **55**, 189-237.
20. Hearne, K.M.T. (1989) *Visions of the Future*. Aquarian Press, Wellingborough, Northants.
21. Hearne, K.M.T. (1982) An ostensible precognition of the 1974 Flixborough disaster. *Journal of the Society for Psychical Research*, **51** (790), 210-13.
22. Price, H.H. (1949) Psychical research and human personality. *The Hibbert Journal*, **47**, 105-13 (p109).

The Author

Dr Keith Hearne is the world's leading researcher into 'lucid' dreaming—and a remarkable pioneer. In the sleep-laboratory in 1975, he obtained the first eye-movement signals from a subject having a lucid dream, and discovered the basic physiological characteristics of lucid dreaming in an extensive study. He then went on to discover the first consistent effect within the dream—the 'light-switch' phenomenon—and even invented and patented the 'dream machine'—a device that can be used by people at home to increase dream recall and experimentally induce dream lucidity.

Dr Hearne received an Honours degree in Psychology from Reading University in 1973, a Master's degree in Psychology from Hull University in 1975, and a Ph.D. (the first on lucid dreaming) from Liverpool University in 1978. Subsequently, he worked for the Medical Research Council, and set up a Research Organization. He has written many scientific papers and articles.

In addition to sleep and dream research, Dr Hearne is an expert in parapsychology and has written a book on his findings in that area. Another book concerns aspects of death and the possibilities of continuing consciousness. He also writes various types of music and is a prolific inventor.

Dr Hearne has appeared many times on TV and radio in several different countries, talking about his areas of expertise.

Index

By the same author

Visions of the Future

The definitive study of premonitions

Many people experience premonitions, yet little research has been carried out to determine exactly what they are, how they occur and how reliable they can be. The author investigates this fascinating subject and comes up with some startling discoveries.

Starting with an account of premonitions throughout recorded history, he proceeds to an in-depth study of contemporary cases. By authenticating and examining up-to-date accounts, he concludes that scientists are being unscientific by refusing to acknowledge this valid area of parapsychology.

A revolutionary new theory is suggested to explain the clear-cut evidence for premonitions but which challenges the modern scientific view of the universe as a material reality.